Beyond AA
Dealing Responsibly
With Alcohol

By

Clarence Barrett

Positive Attitudes, Publishers
Eugene, Oregon 97402-9122

i

Beyond AA
Dealing Responsibly
With Alcohol

Clarence Barrett

Published by: POSITIVE ATTITUDES, Publishers
87344 Prince Lane
Eugene, OR 97402-9122

Library of Congress Catalog Card Number: 95-071989

ISBN 0-9630292-9-0

CONTENTS

ACKNOWLEDGMENTS

The author wishes to express his gratitude to his friend and mentor, Dr. William Glasser, for his encouragement and guidance from the beginning of the preparation of the First Edition of this book and continuing until the present date. Thanks is also due Neil H. McNaughton, Executive Director of Serenity Lane Treatment Center for Alcohol and Drug Dependency, for his support and timely suggestions. And the invaluable help of Sonja Nelson in proofreading and correcting the manuscript must certainly be acknowledged.

FOREWORD

While this book was obviously written for the drinking person, I believe alcohol counselors and therapists, as well as the abusers of other substances, can benefit from reading it.

A recent announcement by the National Institute on Drug Abuse ranked current drugs in the order of their likelihood to create dependency on their use. Alcohol, which many are not used to thinking of as a "drug" at all, was ranked ahead of heroin, cocaine, marijuana, PCP, LSD and caffeine. It was preceded only by crack cocaine, Valium and, of all things, nicotine — the active ingredient in cigarettes and cigars and the most addictive of all drugs.

Perhaps ironically our culture, our legal system and our government have made freely available to the public (with rare exceptions) three of the four most addictive substances known to man: nicotine in cigarette dispensing machines and at grocery counters nationwide, Valium from easy-to-get prescriptions (you usually only need tell your physician you are tense or under stress, and who isn't?) and alcohol from state owned dispensaries or ordinary grocery and drug stores in most states, to say nothing of night clubs, restaurants and neighborhood taverns.

The current "war on drugs" focuses mainly on heroin, cocaine, "crack", marijuana, LSD, and methamphetamines for, after all, they are the illegal drugs and the drugs we have in our culture been taught to abhor, to fear, to distrust, to associate with organized crime and violence. In an earlier "war", Congress passed and the states ratified the 18th amendment to the U. S. Constitution, prohibiting the manufacture, sale, distribution or transportation of alcoholic beverages in an effort to eradicate the scourge of alcoholism. Of course it didn't work because the people in this country didn't want to do away with this wonder drug that provided so much pleasure and suppressed so much pain, and soon the 18th amendment was repealed. With the exception of a few isolated areas that still prohibit the sale of alcohol, it is now very freely available.

While the war on drugs doesn't much concern itself with alcohol, other more exotic, illegal drugs being its primary focus, alcohol addiction has historically caused and continues to cause more broken marriages and families, more loss of time from jobs, more automobile accidents with resulting injuries and deaths, and perhaps more wasted lives, ruined health, heartache and grief than any other addiction. Yet this perfectly legal drug, used responsibly, can be the source of pleasure and relaxation, a social lubricant and conversational tool — even a health adjunct in very moderate quantities according to some physicians.

It is apparent that alcohol will be with us for some time to come so it behooves us to learn to live with it, but in order to do so we need to know what it is, what it does to our bodies and minds, how to avoid problems that can arise from its consumption and, if problems have already arisen, how to deal responsibly with those problems and proceed to live a happy and productive life. That is exactly what this book is all about.

Descriptions of the different forms of potable alcohol are set forth in easy to understand terms including their approximate alcoholic content. A valuable table is included which reveals the blood alcohol content of the average person after consuming various quantities of alcohol, and the effects one can expect to experience from those concentrations. This information is indispensable to the person attempting to learn controlled drinking, the techniques for which are spelled out in some detail in Chapter X.

But controlled drinking does not work for everyone. For a great many people the first drink leads to many more and to a loss of control. For those people the only realistic answer is total abstinence — no alcohol whatever, in any form.

A chapter is included which reviews many of the treatment methods that have historically been tried by researchers and therapists in their often futile efforts to limit or eliminate alcohol consumption by their patients. An entire chapter is devoted to the history, philosophy and workings of Alcoholics Anonymous, revealing it for what it truly is, a valuable support group that helps many people, but by no means everyone, with its share of legends and limitations — even failures.

Throughout this work a couple of valuable concepts are emphasized time and again: (1) That people generally do what they really want to do and avoid doing what they don't want to do and (2) That people always choose their behaviors, including drinking behaviors. These are very important principles when dealing with alcohol problems for they indicate that it is not likely a substance abuser will suddenly stop abusing unless that is what he or she really wants to do, but that the excessive drinking is a chosen behavior and that the drinking person, given the proper motivation, could make a more responsible choice.

In other words, responsibility for the excessive drinking behavior is placed exactly where it belongs — on the drinking person who, of course, is the only one in the world who can do anything about it. And he **can** do something about it, contrary to the philosophy so prevalent in our modern permissive society that the alcoholic is a victim of circumstances beyond his control, and that he cannot by will alone control his drinking. As Barrett states, in the end the drinker's will power and determination are about the only things we have to work with.

So the common dogmas in the treatment of alcoholism: conditioning by electrical or chemical aversive therapy, prolonged free association and counseling procedures, inquiries into the subject's life history, referral to Alcoholics Anonymous as a treatment modality rather than merely a support group, the concept that alcoholics cannot control their drinking— all are minimized in favor of the more pragmatic concepts of Reality Therapy: that all the alcoholic is doing is trying to satisfy certain of his basic needs, needs that are shared by all human beings, but is doing so irresponsibly and needs to be taught more responsible ways.

This book undertakes to teach those ways and does so in a personal, empathetic fashion. Further, it contains an abbreviated review of alcohol treatment methods, a revelation of the true workings of Alcoholics Anonymous that may give even the experienced therapist some pause, and to some, a refreshing introduction to a relatively new but effective approach to treatment. All in all I believe it is about the best book on alcoholism that I have read.

William Glasser, M.D.
Canoga Park, California
June, 1991

FOREWORD TO REVISED EDITION

Having carefully read the Revised Edition of this book, I believe that adding the additional material on control theory adds substantially to what the author has to say. Basically life is a matter of a great series of choices. Control theory gives the basis for the choices. The hardest thing for people to grasp is that in the end we have to choose what we do. Unfortunately many people addicted to alcohol and other drugs die before they learn to make the right choices. This book should help to avert such tragedies.

William Glasser, M.D.
Chatsworth, California
January, 1996

PREFACE

I was born and raised in a small town in the Midwest where the use of alcohol was accepted by and the recreation of choice of the vast majority of adults. In an era before the introduction of television and in a town of 300 people without a theater or other recreational facility there was little else to do. Alcohol abuse was frequent and often resulted in fighting and domestic violence but was tolerated. The operator of the local liquor store sold illegally but openly to teenagers, and even those who had not reached their teen years could usually acquire liquor through the services of the town drunk, who would make the purchase in exchange for a drink of the contents. My first purchase of whiskey was made in this manner and the price turned out to be almost half the contents of the pint bottle. The town drunk had a remarkable thirst. I was twelve years old at the time and the year was 1936.

Some of my earliest memories are of the periodic binges in which my father engaged. It happened that he had an extremely low tolerance for alcohol and a single drink of hard liquor or bottle of beer would soon be very obvious in his behavior and appearance. I used to say that I could tell if he had had a single drink when I was close enough to recognize that he was my father. Three drinks would result in his staggering and wetting his pants and a fifth or sixth drink would often put him to sleep. By spacing them out he often managed to drink more and to make an entire evening or holiday unpleasant for everyone. My mother, of course, was violently opposed to my father's drinking and was very vocal in her opposition so his drinking episodes, while brief, were always traumatic for the family.

Alcohol, while frequently a part of my life up to and including the World War II years, did not really present any problem other than an occasional headache or hangover, although at times I became concerned enough to limit my consumption and even, on a couple of occasions, to eliminate alcohol entirely for periods of six months to a year.

Family and personal finances were such that I would never have been able to attend college except for the advent of the G. I. Bill. In 1953 I graduated from the University of Oregon with a Bachelor of Science degree and in 1955 was awarded the degree, Doctor of Jurisprudence (J. D.). My choice of law as a career was purely fortuitous so it was not surprising that I did not find the practice particularly rewarding, except in a monetary sense. I had acquired a fairly good background in the humanities during my undergraduate years so I was able to do some counseling with clients concerning their personal, as well as their legal problems. This inevitably led me into the area of alcohol counseling from time to time, a somewhat frustrating experience since I was not then prepared to deal with such matters in any depth.

During my law school days alcohol became an increasingly important part of my life. I'm not sure of the reason, although I surmise it had something to do with the drastic change of circumstances in my life in moving from a laboring class background to an association with upper middle class professionals. This was not an easy transition for me and I was almost constantly ill at ease in social situations. Alcohol, of course, alleviated this condition considerably. On one occasion, as chairman of the entertainment committee of a local service club, I acted as master of ceremonies for a program presented before an audience of hundreds of people, a feat I would never have undertaken at all had I not been intoxicated. It seemed to me at the time that I did an outstanding job, although I can't speak for the audience.

Upon graduating from law school I was employed by a small law firm, two partners of which were alcohol abusers. Down the hall were two other attorneys, both excessive drinkers, and the occupants of the two offices frequently got together in the afternoons for drinking activities. They were often joined by others and a party usually ensued. One of the attorneys had no children or other family responsibilities so was well able to afford all the liquor he wanted and he offered me booze for companionship, an exchange I was happy to make at the time. I had the habit and not the money while he had both. From that time until February 1, 1959, a period of approximately four years, I did not spend a single twenty four hour period without being intoxicated to some degree. The drinking usually began about eleven o'clock in the morning and continued through the day and evening and often until the small hours of the next morning. Fortunately during all this time I was able to present myself clean shaven and well dressed during the usual morning office hours and was able to spend at least a few hours each day taking care of business affairs. I frequently had the thought that I should not be doing what I was doing; that I knew better; that I was ruining my health and my life and perhaps, in fact probably, having a negative influence on the rest of my family, although somehow the bills got paid and the family was properly fed and dressed.

It was my custom, before going to the office in the morning, to stop in an early bar nearby for my breakfast, consisting of a double vodka martini. This was usually served in a champagne glass and it gradually became more and more difficult to get it up to my mouth without embarrassing myself. Finally, on February 1, 1959, after trying unsuccessfully for twenty minutes to raise the champagne glass to my lips without spilling the contents I reluctantly asked the bartender to pour the drink into a water tumbler, whereupon I drank it and went to my office as usual. Then I recall sitting for an hour or so contemplating recent events and deciding simply that I wanted never to drink alcohol again — I had had enough. I haven't had alcohol in any form since that morning.

Since retiring from my law practice at the age of fifty years I have lived on a farm near the University of Oregon and have had time to resume my studies in the fields of psychology and sociology with emphasis on the subject of alcohol abuse. I also had the good fortune to spend a period of time studying with William Glasser, psychiatrist, author and originator of Reality Therapy, a concept of phychotherapy that seems to have a great potential for treatment of substance abusers. It has also been a tremendous learning experience to have been active in the formation, operation and direction of a living unit for alcoholics. In this and other positions I have counseled many alcoholics, individually and in groups of five to eight, and have attended many meetings of Alcoholics Anonymous.

A great deal of research has been done over the years in the field of alcohol abuse, most of which has concerned itself with the causes, nature, extent and treatment of alcoholism and alcohol abuse. Much of it is redundant, a great deal of it is difficult to understand and interpret, little of it seems to have much practical applicability to everyday life and not much of it is easily accessible to the lay person who needs it, since it reposes in technical and scholarly journals, books and reports. It is my hope that I may, through means of this work, bring to the lay person in usable form some of the relevant and meaningful portions of this vast accumulation of knowledge so that it may be considered and perhaps put to some practical use. It is my further hope that drinking persons who have been considering attempts to change their drinking behaviors will now proceed , and my ultimate hope that alcohol abusers who may in the past have tried abstinence and failed, may be inspired to try again — and succeed.

This book is not intended as a scholarly work (there are already so many of those in the libraries) but rather as a message of hope to those with drinking or other substance abuse problems, from someone who has "been there". It is hoped that the brief bibliography will not frighten people into thinking of this as a text book — it is only appended to give sources of further reading materials to those who may wish to consider the present state of alcohol studies and the attempts that have been made and are being made to deal with alcoholism.

It has not been easy to determine the effectiveness of alcohol and substance abuse treatment programs. There have not as yet developed adequate criteria for scientifically judging their worth but the studies that have been done have pretty largely concluded that present methods of treatment are just not very effective. [1,2] Meanwhile, each modality claims its share of successes and continues to limp along, frequently with the conviction that if only more money were available its program could be expanded and would thus be more effective. Diane M. Riley and others, in 1987, after an exhaustive review and comparison of alcohol treatment studies, concluded that since no current treatment works very well perhaps our efforts should be directed to developing an alternative treatment with a demonstrable effectiveness. [3]

You will find in this book brief descriptions of some of the past and current treatment methods that have seemed to work for some people some of the time and an occasional comment on their shortcomings as viewed by this writer. These descriptions are not intended to be exhaustive, nor is the list complete, as there are many variations in the treatment methods mentioned, but they are intended to give some idea to the uninitiated of the nature of alcohol treatment concepts available to them. The final chapters contain some suggestions that it is believed will work for you, if you **really want** to change your drinking behaviors.

While this work is primarily directed to those with an actual or potential alcohol problem, the concepts and techniques described apply equally well to other fields of substance abuse.

Modern literature and experience indicates that the problems of alcoholism know no gender boundaries, so where the masculine gender is used in the text it could as well be the feminine and vice versa, except for direct references to specific persons.

C. B.

INTRODUCTION TO SECOND EDITION

Persons who are addicted to alcohol or other drugs are generally persons whose lives are out of control. This book is intended as a self-help manual to assist them is regaining control. The original edition touched lightly on the concepts of William Glasser's *Control Theory*, but in today's social climate these ideas have assumed tremendous new importance in countering the victim status and role of helplessness assumed by so many people. Applications of control theory have therefore been greatly expanded in this revised edition.

With this major change, the basic thrust of the book remains the same: we choose our behaviors, bad or good, and have the ability to change from non-productive, destructive behaviors to those that better meet our basic needs.

A recent book by Mark B. and Linda C. Sobell, *Problem Drinkers: Guided Self-Change Treatment* (1993, The Guilford Press, NY) summarizes various research outcomes that indicate there is no difference in the success ratios of outpatient treatment as opposed to inpatient treatment, particularly when dealing with problem drinkers rather than more seriously dependent drinkers. Furthermore, their studies showed that those problem drinkers using self-help manuals, such as this book, fared as well as those in either form of treatment. If you are a problem drinker, give this book a good try before seeking a more expensive, more intensive regimen. It can help you take control of your life. This is the only life you are going to have, at least on this earth, so make the most of it.

C.B., Eugene, Oregon, 1996.

CHOICES

Do you have a drinking problem?

If you can read and understand this paragraph you are capable of taking the first steps toward controlling your drinking or toward permanent, total sobriety, since there is no other acceptable form of sobriety for many alcohol abusers.

Stop and think about that before you read on. Is that what **you** want? Not what your spouse wants or your employer wants or your family or friends want or what a court has mandated you to do, but what **you** want? It doesn't matter why you want it. It may be because you'll be sent to jail if you do not, or because your spouse threatens to leave and divorce you and take the kids if you do not, or simply because you have decided that a chemical substance should no longer control your life. What does matter is that **you** want control over your drinking or permanent, total sobriety. And you can have it! This book was created to assist you. It is a self-help manual.

I once had a friend who became aware that his body, at forty years of age, was becoming flabby and losing its usual agility and elasticity. He belonged to a local service club that provided a well equipped gym for its members so he embarked

1

on a regular exercise program and was soon in excellent physical condition from working out with weights and elaborate exercise machines and participating in handball, racquetball and other competitive games. The program was so popular the service club decided to enlarge its facilities and found it necessary to close the gym temporarily for construction purposes. My friend, deprived temporarily of the elaborate facilities, abandoned his exercise program until the remodelling was complete.

When the gym again became available three weeks later it was with some new use restriction. Certain areas and facilities were available to certain groups only at certain times, an arrangement which didn't suit my friend's convenience, so his exercise program was further postponed until his schedule could be worked out. Somehow this rescheduling never materialized so the exercise program was abandoned and my friend's body, at forty-one years of age, was once again flabby and without its former agility and elasticity, but he had a host of reasons for its being beyond his control: the temporary closure of the gym messed up his schedule, the new policies of the club made it impossible for him to take up his activities again, and so on. With his luck I guess the poor guy is doomed to a life of flab, right? WRONG! Obviously there were a great many things he could have done while the gym was being remodelled to keep his body in trim. To name a few, he could have jogged, done isometric exercises, swum in a public pool, climbed mountains, did calisthenics, gone for walks or even just jumped up and down. So why didn't he keep his body in condition as he well knew he should have done, by his own admission? **Because he didn't want to.**

I used to smoke cigarettes, unfiltered, king sized, a real man's cigarette, three packs a day, day after day, year after year. I lied quite a bit to my mother, my wife and others who cared.

I said I lit them without realizing it and mostly they just burned up in the ash tray. Baloney! I always knew when I lit one, and I smoked them right down to where they started to burn my lips, inhaling every puff. When working in my shop or at building or in the garden or in the kitchen or my office — anyplace where my hands were used — the cigarette hung from my lips, smoke curling into my nostrils, my eyes smarting and burning, and the eyes and nostrils of my clients and friends likewise undoubtedly smarting and burning.

You'd think I'd have gotten tired of the inconvenience if nothing else, and the outright physical discomfort, to say nothing of my awareness of the discomfort of clients and friends. You're right, and I quit, for about a year. But one beautiful spring morning some friends invited me over for coffee at their lawn table and of course the inevitable pack of cigarettes lay open upon the table, king sized filters this time. So I had one with my coffee and it tasted so good that I bought a pack (just one) on the way home. Bingo! Back to three packs a day, day after day, year after year, eyes and nostrils smarting.

But my annual physical examination revealed no apparent problems. A vital capacity test indicated my lungs were fantastically efficient. The technician who administered the test actually asked me what brand I smoked, a seeming endorsement of what I had been doing. The statistical chances of my developing lung cancer from smoking were only about six in one hundred thousand, a relatively insignificant threat to a confirmed smoker, and my heart was strong as an ox. Although not plagued with hacking coughs, heart murmurs, poor appetite, loss of taste or smell or any other obvious symptom of smoking abuse, I kept having the nagging thought that this thing was controlling me and for some reason that was unacceptable. So I quit smoking again, this time suffering such withdrawal symptoms as one reads about in connection with heroin withdrawal. That was over twenty five years ago and I haven't smoked since. Why was I able to quit smoking in the face of such agonizing discomfort? **Because I really wanted to.**

As this is written Thanksgiving has just passed and Christmas is not far off — both traditional feast days in my particular culture. I love to eat and I'm a pretty good cook. Our family produces most of what we eat and can afford the rest. With three freezers, a cellar and a pantry full of food, why not eat? I do, frequently and with gusto. Not only is the taste of food enjoyed as it is chewed and swallowed but the very act of eating is somehow satisfying and pleasurable, aside from the knowledge that it is nourishing my body and providing the strength to move about and carry on my life.

I've also noticed that larger and fancier meals are prepared if someone is going to eat with me. There is an element of conviviality in eating with friends and family even on ordinary days, let alone feast days, so more is eaten then than if I'm alone. Then, of course, there is the race to the refrigerator during TV commercials, the impulsive purchase of chocolate bars and nuts while grocery shopping, the between meals invitations from neighbors for pie and coffee. I just don't seem to be able to say "no" and stick with it.

So, am I a blimp? Fortunately not, for my body chemistry is such that it manages to turn most of the food consumed into heat and energy rather than fat, although trousers with a thirty-eight waist lately feel more comfortable than the old thirty-sixes worn for years. But what is the processing of all that food doing to my internal organs and my body chemistry? I've read many times that overeating tends to shorten one's life and I certainly want to live to be an old and healthy person. So, why keep eating so much, knowing full well it is probably shortening my life? Because I'm a glutton (There, it's been said!). But having said I'm a glutton I've succeeded in labeling myself as one of those people who have a problem they really can't do much about, a victim of circumstances beyond my control— a "sickness," really. I'm just doomed to a shortened life so might as well give up. Oh, of course, something heroic could be done like checking out Overeaters Anonymous or some appetite control pills could be obtained but everyone knows these are temporary, ineffective stopgaps. Besides, Aunt Elizabeth ate like a horse, weighed 380 pounds and lived to be eighty-six. Maybe I'll get lucky like that. Anyway, that's a long way off. Meanwhile, there's that delicious pecan pie in the pantry.

I'm an intelligent person, able to assimilate facts easily and understand the logical and probable consequences of over-eating. I've read in magazine articles that I may have a compulsion that probably has its roots in early childhood, perhaps an oral fixation. So, knowing I have a problem and that it is probably taking me to an early grave, having some idea what causes the problem and knowing full well what to do about it, why do I continue to eat too much? Simple: **Because I want to. I choose** to eat more than I should, just as I **chose** to start smoking, and later to stop it, and just as my friend **chose** to stop exercising even though he knew he'd return to a flabby condi-tion as a result. Furthermore, my friend and I found abundant reasons to justify our choices, valid or not.

Webster's Third International Dictionary defines **"de-termination"** thusly: "....fixed resolution....the power or habit of deciding definitely and firmly; ability to persist against opposition or attempts to dissuade or discourage....", and **"re-solve"** as follows: "....to determine after reflection: as, on a better course of life." **"Volition"** is "the act of willing or choosing: the act of deciding (as on a course of action or an end to be striven for): the exercise of the will....", and **"willpower"** is "....the power of controlling one's own actions or emotions: self-control, self-direction....the power of choosing and of acting in accordance with choice." [4]

For many years it has been unfashionable to mention the word **"willpower"** in the context of alcohol abuse, and particularly in connection with any treatment modality. Usually it has been summarily dismissed as moralistic, simplistic or naive. Yet, if there is a common thread that connects all treatment approaches in the field of alcohol abuse it is that the drinkers must be persuaded, coerced, motivated or conditioned to change their behavior from drinking to abstinence or at least controlled drinking. Such changes have historically proven difficult to accomplish and largely temporary unless volitional on the part of the drinker. Volitional change would seem to connote a decision on the part of the drinker and the exercise of resolve, of some power of self-determination or self-direction — perhaps the exercise of **willpower.**

The power of the human will, even that of the common drunk, is legendary. Consider for instance the cunning, resourcefulness, determination and self-direction demonstrated by skid row drinkers in securing their daily requirement of wine. Begging, conning, panhandling, mugging, shoplifting, prostituting, and even working, are some of the common pursuits utilized by such drinkers in their determination or will to continue their drinking behavior.

At the opposite end of the economic scale, consider the determination and will required by the wealthy alcohol abusing dowager to surreptitiously secure a steady supply of liquor via cabbies and grocery or liquor store operators and to successfully hide the consumption of large quantities of liquor from family, friends, household employees, the family doctor and others.

Perhaps more usual and closer to the experience of the average person is the example of the factory worker, millworker or construction worker who directs his determination and will to the economic problem of insuring a secure supply of alcohol to satisfy his or her habit while attempting to adequately support the family and perhaps children of a previous marriage that has ended in divorce.

There would seem to be little question as to the **power** of human determination and will to direct and control the course of human behavior, the challenge being to direct or guide the problem drinker's determination and will toward constructive rather than destructive ends. Of course it is ineffective to tell alcohol abusers they keep failing in their attempts to control alcohol because they "don't have enough will power." This, indeed, is not only moralistic but judgmental as well and certainly wouldn't do much for their self esteem. The fact is, they have **plenty of will power** and have just been misdirecting it.

Society, represented by its sociologists, psychologists, physicians, ministers, lawmakers and police, has been unable to effectively define the problem, let alone formulate any meaningful, consistent or workable plan of action. Every discipline has its favorite theory of causation from time to time, and each has had its approach to treatment. Perhaps because human behavior is an ever changing phenomenon, quite incapable of real objective measurement or scientific method, there has been little agreement except as to the futility of most treatment methods over the long pull. It has been suggested by some people in the field that most alcohol abusers who seemed to be helped by treatment were probably predisposed to changing their drinking behavior **before** going into therapy.

Once the alcohol abuser is detoxified and restored to a mental state conducive to rational thought, the ultimate goal of every entity that deals with the problems of alcohol abuse is, or should be, to attempt to motivate the alcohol abuser to make a firm decision to change his or her drinking behavior and to act on that decision with resolve and commitment. This process cannot effectively take place in a milieu that bombards the drinker with information that discourages the exercise of determination, resolve, volition, willpower. After all, in the end these are about the only things we have to work with.

It is readily apparent that there are many problem drinkers who cannot or will not be motivated to exercise their determination and will toward a change in their drinking behaviors. Many alcoholics go into treatment for the sole purpose of getting their body restored to good health so they can get back to some serious drinking. But there are many others who are motivated and have tried various treatment methods and failed, or worse, have been discouraged from bothering to try at all. This is tragic, and totally unnecesary. They must be taught that it is within their power to control this scourge — that they, and only they, have the power to do so.

ALCOHOL

Many works dealing with alcohol abuse emphasize the statistical relationships between alcohol and traffic deaths, causal relationships between alcohol consumption and various heart, liver and other bodily dysfunctions, as well as descriptions of alcohol's effect on the body chemistry, even when ingested in small amounts. One wonders if these matters are meaningful to the average drinking person, if it really serves any purpose to rehash them. A man in one of my group therapy sessions disclosed to the group that after watching his favorite uncle die painfully of cirrhosis of the liver after many years of alcohol abuse, he went out and got drunk. His uncle's experience with alcohol apparently meant little.

People have been brewing, drinking and abusing alcohol throughout recorded history, and probably before. The author once read an account of the unearthing of a brewery dating back 5,400 years in the ancient city of Hierakonpolis (William Booth in Washington Post.) It is and will be as much a part of our culture, our life, as air and water. Some of it tastes good, all of it feels good, and it serves a purpose: it entertains, it eases pain, it builds courage, it frees inhibitions, it lubricates conversation, it relaxes, it soothes, it gives pleasure. It is a very useful substance. Most people use it appropriately; only relatively few abuse it.

Most drinkers are aware that excessive consumption of alcohol is not in their best interests, but it is questionable whether that knowledge profoundly influences their judgment as other pressures encourage them to overindulge. How many people who sit in a bar enjoying a few drinks with their friends after work consciously consider that they may die or kill someone else in a traffic accident on the way home? Yet it happens — a lot. How many people, happily toasting the bride and groom at a wedding reception are conscious of the sometimes devastating chemical reactions then going on within their bodies? Few, if any. It is human nature to expect tragedy to befall others, not us. And body chemistry is something for the concern of the laboratory, strangely beyond our comprehension or belief.

The author once attended a series of night classes in a junior college setting, taught by staff members of a private, non-profit alcohol education and counseling organization. Stressed were the physical, psychological, social, and legal implications of alcohol abuse. With few exceptions the twenty or so students were there because they were already exhibiting symptoms of problem drinking. In age they appeared to range from late teens to middle thirties. Many were attending by mandate of a court as a condition of their probation or parole for some alcohol related offense; others were attending as part of their therapy in connection with an alcohol treatment facility. At least one attended in compliance with the sentence of a federal court, and some went to earn college credit. The lectures were, for the most part, poorly organized and presented, and the reaction of the students was pure boredom.

But who knows what seeds may have been planted, perhaps to germinate and grow years hence? Scientists are baffled at the newfound incidence of apparently spontaneous remissions, even among those for years exhibiting symptoms of extreme problem drinking. Perhaps these remissions, if all were known, were not so spontaneous but resulted from an accumulation of small learning experiences and bits of knowledge observed only peripherally, and finally triggered by some life crisis.

Just what is alcohol, anyway? Chemically it is any one of a whole class of compounds: **methanol or methyl alcohol,** sometimes known as wood alcohol, which is an industrial solvent and is not potable; **isopropyl or rubbing alcohol,** which is a disinfectant and not suitable for drinking; and **ethanol or ethyl alcohol** which differs from the other forms in that it may be consumed and is the basic ingredient in intoxicants referred to commonly as alcoholic beverages. It is ethanol that will be referred to throughout this work whenever the word "alcohol" is used. It doesn't matter what form the beverage may take — beer, wine, gin, whiskey, vodka or whatever — if it is drinkable it contains **ethanol** and no other form of alcohol.

Ethanol is a product of the fermentation of fruits or grains. The enzymes or yeasts that convert the plant sugars into alcohol through the fermentation process cannot survive in ethanol concentrations of more than 14% so wines and beers cannot exceed 14% unless they are distilled or fortified by adding more ethanol. Alcohol has a lower boiling point than water, the other major ingredient in most brews; thus wines, beers and other fermented solutions, sometimes called mash, may be heated to just above the boiling point of alcohol, and the alcohol vapors condensed in cooling coils to form a relatively pure alcohol solution. Beverage alcohol is not usually available in its pure form. Rather, enough water is added to reduce its strength to 50% or less. A 50% solution of alcohol is stated as "100 proof ".

Wines are fermented from a variety of fruits, grapes being the most common historically, although other fruits have gained in popularity. Enough alcohol to increase the content to about 20% is sometimes added, in which case the wine is said to be fortified. Unfortified wines are usually called table wines. Beer results from the fermentation of malted grains such as corn, barley, wheat or rye. The fermentation process is stopped before the alcohol content exceeds 3% to 6%. Dried hops are added for flavor. Ale is made in a somewhat similar manner, but the alcohol content is usually somewhat higher than that of beer.

Various types of whiskcy, scotch, bourbon and rye being the most common, are made by distilling the fermented juices of cereal grains. Gin is a combination of alcohol and water to which various flavors have been added, such as juniper, lemon or orange. Vodka results from the distillation of either fermented potatoes or grains. It is almost colorless, odorless and tasteless and for this reason is often favored for "inconspicuous" drinking on the erroneous assumption that it is not noticeable on one's breath.

Brandy is distilled from wines. Certain types of brandy, such as cognac, are named for the area in which the fruit is grown. Sometimes sugar and flavorings are added to brandy to create liqueur, a dessert beverage having an alcohol content of 20% to 65%. Rum is distilled from fermented molasses or sugar cane juice. Some other alcoholic beverages in less common use in this country are: meade, a fermented honey solution; sake, a Japanese rice wine; and tequila, a Mexican beverage made by distilling fermented cactus juice.

Obviously some beverages have a higher alcohol content than others, and it is the alcohol content, not the name or taste, that creates the effect on the person drinking it. For example, twelve ounces of beer, four ounces of wine and one ounce of whiskey all have about the same alcohol content. This is very important to remember because this is the amount of alcohol that the average 150-pound person can metabolize in one hour. If such person drank only one drink per hour it is not likely he would feel much effect. Of course a smaller person would metabolize a proportionately smaller amount of alcohol in an hour, while a larger person would metabolize proportionately more.

If more alcohol is consumed than the body can metabolize, the excess remains in the bloodstream to affect the brain and various other organs of the body. The effects are directly related to the percentage of alcohol in the blood, called blood alcohol concentration or BAC.

The following is a chart showing the approximate BAC of people of various body weights as a result of consuming drinks of one ounce of 100 proof liquor, twelve ounces of beer or four ounces of table wine. Detachable copies of this chart may be found at the end of this book.

Drinks   **Body weight in pounds**

	100	120	140	160	180	200	220	240
1	.04	.03	.03	.02	.02	.02	.02	.02
2	.08	.06	.05	.05	.04	.04	.03	.03
3	.11	.09	.08	.07	.06	.06	.05	.05
4	.15	.12	.11	.09	.08	.08	.07	.06
5	.19	.16	.13	.12	.11	.09	.09	.08
6	.23	.19	.16	.14	.13	.11	.10	.09
7	.26	.22	.19	.16	.15	.13	.12	.11
8	.30	.25	.21	.19	.17	.15	.14	.13
9	.34	.26	.24	.21	.19	.17	.15	.14
10	.38	.31	.27	.23	.21	.19	.17	.16

These figures anticipate the consumption of the listed amounts within one hour so you may deduct .01% BAC for each forty minutes of drinking time, this being the amount normally metabolized by the average body during that time.

At a BAC of 0.03% the average person will feel relaxed and slightly exhilarated; at 0.06% reaction time will be slowed, muscle control will be poor, speech slightly slurred and legs a little wobbly; at 0.09% judgment will be clouded, inhibitions lessened, ability to reason and make logical decisions impaired. At a BAC of 0.12% the average person's vision will be blurred, speech unclear, walking unsteady and coordination impaired; at 0.15% all behavior will be impaired and it will be difficult to stay awake; at 0.30% semi stupor occurs, or perhaps deep sleep; and at 0.50% the person is in a deep stupor and in danger of death. At a BAC of 1% the part of the brain that controls the automatic body functions such as heart beat and breathing becomes inoperative and death occurs. In many states a BAC of 0.10% is sufficient evidence that a person is under the influence of alcohol to the extent that he is not capable of operating a motor vehicle safely, while in some states 0.08% is sufficient.

Since the body continues to metabolize alcohol even while the drinking is going on, it is obviously important to consider the time period over which the alcohol is consumed. Six drinks consumed over a period of three hours would not be as intoxicating as the same amount consumed over a period of one hour since during the three hour drinking period the average 150 pound body would have burned up three of the drinks, leaving only three remaining in the bloodstream to affect the brain. Consider, then, the effect of consumption of, say, twenty-eight ounces of liquor within a few seconds, such as a person "chugging" a fifth of vodka or whiskey in a show of bravado. All the alcohol reaches the bloodstream at once, with no chance for the body to metabolize even a small portion. Death often results unless immediate medical attention is made available. This happens many times each year, particularly among inexperienced young drinkers.

Alcohol is not a stimulant as many people are inclined to think because they feel euphoric and "stimulated" when they drink. Rather it is a depressant — it tends to slow you down, to anesthetize. Sedatives, muscle relaxants and tranquilizers like Valium and Librium are also depressants. Therefore it is particularly dangerous to consume alcohol at the same time these chemicals are in your system. The net effect, rather than being merely additive, is in fact multiplying. That is to say, the total effect is often many times greater than would be the effect of just the alcohol or other chemical alone and can, in fact, be lethal.

The drugs which most violently react with alcohol include, in addition to Valium and Librium, barbiturates of all types, including Seconal, Nembutal and Tuinal and their generic counterparts, which are made by many drug manufacturers; quaaludes, Sopors, Mandrax and other methaqualone drugs; Thorazine, Stellazine, Miltown, Equanil, Elavil, Triavil and most others among the tranquilizers and tricyclic anti-depressants; PCP (Phencyclidine) or "Angel Dust."

If you suspect an overdose possibility, whether from alcohol alone or in combination with other drugs, get medical help as soon as possible. Do not simply allow the person to sleep it off. He may suffer heart or respiratory failure. The author once went to the apartment of a client who had failed to appear for an important court appearance and found him in bed, drowned in his own vomit after over indulgence in alcohol.

Traditional "cures" for alcohol overindulgence, such as cold showers and copious quantities of hot coffee, are of no value whatsoever. Nor is there any way to speed up the body's normal rate of disposing of alcohol, about one drink per hour. Only time will do the job and a "hangover" seems to be the unavoidable price one must pay for overindulgence.

ALCOHOLISM

A very dear friend we will call Sam, was an excellent attorney when he was sober, which was most of the time. But in the thirty years I knew him he went from a handsome, personable young law student with two tiny children and a lovely wife who adored him to an anxious, overweight, alcohol abuser without a wife, home, office, library or profession, to death at age fifty eight from a heart condition brought on by acute alcoholism. Sam was a periodic drunk. He would go for approximately three to six months without a drink, working long hours, devoting his spare time to gardening and woodworking, with an occasional game of golf. He loved good music, good food, good companionship and nice things.

Sometimes Sam would "get depressed" and go to a psychiatrist acquaintance for counseling and perhaps a pre-scription for Antabuse, a drug that cannot coexist in your system with alcohol without making you very sick. Then one day he'd realize he'd been out of Antabuse and instead of going

17

to the drugstore to renew the prescription he'd head for a bar. He knew exactly what he was doing and what was going to happen, but he didn't care. He was doing what he wanted to do.

During the next two to three weeks Sam's office associates, his secretary, his wife, his creditors, his clients and his friends were at a loss to know what to do. No one knew the status of pending cases. The secretary didn't know what to tell clients when they called, to say nothing of where her next paycheck was coming from. The rent may or may not have gotten paid. Other attorneys were baffled at his failure to return their calls. Utter chaos! But eventually the binge would run its course, and Sam would walk into the office one morning, shaved and well dressed but sick, apologetic, worried, apprehensive, guilt ridden and broke. Everyone pitched in, and somehow the bills got paid, the clients got taken care of, the secretary got pacified, the associates got soothed and the friends placated. Life went on until the next episode.

After each binge Sam seemed so genuinely remorseful, so sincere in his assurances that it wouldn't happen again — that he had finally learned his lesson the hard way — that everyone tended to believe him and to assume that the problem was now behind them at last. What they didn't know, and what Sam was not about to tell them, was that the last thing in the world **he** wanted to do was quit drinking.

Sam went through an aversion therapy clinic twice, outpatient alcohol treatment facilities many times, detoxification facilities countless times. He was jailed a number of times for drunkenness, had his driver's license revoked for drunken driving three times and eventually had his law library and office equipment seized for non payment of income taxes. His first wife gave him countless chances to quit drinking but finally gave up and divorced him, taking an expensive home and all its furnishings in the process. A second marriage ended the same way and for the same reasons after only a very few months. Sam freely admitted that his abuse of alcohol had everything to do with his misfortune.

Now Sam was a very intelligent man and in an effort to appeal to his intelligence the author sat with him during one of his ordeals and asked why he didn't just give up alcohol and thereby solve most of his problems. His reply was immediate and unequivocal: **"Because I don't want to."** Crazy? Maybe not. **He was doing what he wanted to do**. He knew the price he was paying for what he was doing but he still wanted to do it. He would have liked the problems to go away but not enough to give up his beloved alcohol.

Sam tried counseling a few times and even attended a few meetings of Alcoholics Anonymous, but only to pacify others, never because he wanted to change his drinking behaviors. None of it worked for Sam. When he died a few years ago his children scattered his ashes over the Pacific Ocean from an airplane to honor his final wish.

What is alcoholism? Why do we call it that? If someone is hooked on heroin or cocaine we do not refer to their problem as "heroinism" or "cocainism" but as heroin addiction or cocaine addiction. So why not refer to alcohol addiction as exactly that, rather than devising a new name for it: "alcoholism"? Perhaps because the very word "addiction" smacks of illegality and unacceptableness; its connotation is totally negative. Let's face it, of all the addictions in our society alcohol is the most acceptable, and the very substance is legal almost everywhere so we give it a more acceptable name. Once the word "alcoholism" was invented, it is amazing to note the amount of effort that has gone into devising definitions.

As a practicing attorney I was frequently consulted by clients who wanted a divorce or legal separation from a husband or wife because the spouse was an alcoholic. On being pressed for details various clients reported some offending spouses to be consuming a mere six pack of beer a week, others two fifths of hard liquor each day. Frequency of the drinking patterns varied from almost constant consumption during waking hours to periodic binges, separated by sober periods of months or even a year or more.

Offensive behaviors reported ranged from bad breath and snoring through embarrassing social conduct to physical violence, hallucinations, belligerence and coma. Attitudes of the drinkers as reported by their spouses ranged from a nonchalant lack of concern from some, through defiance from others, to an apparent inability to cope with an obsession with alcohol that they abhorred but could not understand or control. One wonders at the almost total lack of any consistent criteria in these lay efforts to define alcoholic behavior.

In reviewing the literature pertaining to alcohol abuse it is interesting to note the number and diversity of scholarly attempts to adequately define alcoholism. The word "alcoholic" was apparently originated by Dr. Thomas Trotter of England and Dr. Benjamin Rush of the United States, prior to 1840. They used the term "alcoholic" interchangeably with the word "drunkard". The American Medical Association has defined alcoholism as "....an illness characterized by preoccupation with alcohol and loss of control over its consumption such as to lead usually to intoxication if drinking is begun; by chronicity; by progression; and by the tendency to relapse,"[5] while Webster defines it as "....continuous and usually excessive use of alcoholic drinks....the state of being poisoned by alcohol; specifically, the pathological results of excessive use of alcoholic drinks...."[6]

Authors, usually with a point of view, have attempted definitions: anyone whose drinking interferes frequently or continuously with any of his important life adjustments and interpersonal relationships;[7]   any use of alcoholic beverages that causes any damage to the individual or society or both;[8] or more expansively, "A chronic and usually progressive disease, or a symptom or an underlying psychological or physical disorder, characterized by dependence on alcohol (manifested by loss of control over drinking) for relief from psychological or physical distress or for gratification from alcohol intoxication itself, and by a consumption of alcoholic beverages sufficiently great and consistent to cause physical or mental or social or economic disability. Or a learned (or conditioned) dependence on alcohol which irresistibly activates resort to alcohol whenever a critical internal or environmental stimulus occurs."[9]

Alcoholics Anonymous, the most noted self-help organization in the field, seems to define alcoholism as loss of the ability to control alcohol, although a clear-cut definition does not seem to appear in its literature. Indirectly it defines it by frequent references to the symptomatology as they see it: a physical allergy to drink; an immature and self-centered "alcoholic personality"; and a "spiritual sickness," that is, the alcoholic's egotistical and self-centered personality prevents any but the most artificial and superficial relations to others or to a "Higher Power".[10] Generally speaking AA encourages the individual to label himself as alcoholic if he feels it is appropriate.

Contemporary writers seem to be avoiding the traditional ritualistic attempts to redefine the terms "alcoholic" and "alcoholism," contenting themselves instead with a free usage of the terms in their usual, functional sense, a most encouraging and appreciated development. After all, we do commonly use many terms effectively in our daily communication, even scientific communication, that are difficult or impossible to define with total objectivity. The need or preference for an objective definition is obviously felt more keenly by researchers and scholars who are attempting to measure, quantify and report their findings in such a way that other researchers and scholars will understand and find the data meaningful and useful.

In describing the classes of drinking behavior I find it convenient to break the entire field into four simple and, except for the first, overlapping categories: (1) abstinence, (2) social drinking, (3) problem drinking and (4) alcoholism. I think the average lay person is used to thinking of alcohol consumption in these common terms.

Abstinence, of course, is total self-denial of alcohol in any form.

Social drinking means the consumption and enjoyment of alcohol to the extent that it does not cause the drinker or anyone else any substantial problem. The drinker may have a little too much on an occasional Saturday night and suffer a mild hangover the next day, may talk a little loudly or too much and be a bit annoying at times but not cause anyone any real problem.

Problem drinking means the consumption of alcohol to the extent or in a manner that results in the drinker or someone else having a problem. Obviously an evening that starts out with social drinking can become an occasion of problem drinking if the drinker gets in a fight, gets arrested for drunken driving, strikes his wife, has an accident with his car, or blacks out. Usually this person realizes the existence of a problem concerning alcohol but can and does exercise a degree of control, at least periodically. Often, **but not always** as some writers would have you believe, the problem drinker's problems become progressively more serious and more frequent until the final stage, alcoholism, is reached.

Alcoholism, by any definition, is problem drinking but in its extreme. Here the drinker may be addicted (have a physical or psychological dependency) to alcohol, may claim to be unable to limit alcohol consumption, may have a variety of physical ailments attributable to alcohol abuse, and is probably preoccupied with a secure supply of alcohol . He may, if the supply is cut off, suffer withdrawal symptoms including delirium tremens (DT's) which may involve disorientation, hallucinations, delusions, impaired consciousness, hypertension, fever and sometimes convulsions.[11] Another very valid derfinition is: (a) the person usually drinks more than the norm for his social group, (b) there are coping problems or adjustment problems as a result of abuse, and (c) loss of control.

These categories are by no means intended to be infallible and any writer, or observer for that matter, might draw lines of demarcation different from those herein and not be in error.

It does not seem reasonable to attempt to fit specific persons into the above categories and thus to label someone as an alcoholic, or a problem drinker. It seems more appropriate to allow the categories to describe patterns of behavior in which certain persons engage from time to time, recognizing that any individual may exhibit characteristics of more than one category at a time and may freely move from one category to another for obvious reasons or for no apparent reason. For example, persons clearly exhibiting behaviors common to social drinking may suddenly develop serious problems in their drinking. Likewise, persons who may have exhibited alcoholic behaviors for years may suddenly and inexplicably stop drinking altogether.

Is alcoholism a disease? The early Christian church considered inebriation to be a sin, voluntary in the sense that it was committed consciously, involuntary in that it arose from man's basic unworthiness. Consequently the early Christian approach to the drinking problem was through spiritual ministrations. Later the church took a less understanding approach and viewed it as a form of possession, and treatment consisted of imprisonment, purges, beatings and other techniques to cleanse the soul.

Prior to 1840 Dr. Trotter of England and Dr. Rush of the U. S. began pressing for more humane treatment of drunkards, whom they called alcoholics. Dr. Trotter was the first doctor to describe excessive drinking as a disease. Excessive drinkers were still considered by the public, including most of the medical profession, to be sinners so the disease concept was not a popular one. Various efforts over the years to achieve disease status for alcoholism steadily won public and professional acceptance until in 1956 the American Medical Association finally classified alcoholism as an illness. But that certainly did not lay the matter to rest and the debate continues to this day.

Proponents of the disease concept list the following in support of their position: the disease label secures for the alcoholic the special care that society reserves for its ill; it gives alcoholic patients the right to dignity and therapy; it firmly establishes alcoholism within the province of the medical profession; it somewhat relieves alcoholics of criminal responsibility for some of their behaviors. Opponents claim that alcoholism is not a disease but a symptom of an inability to make an emotional adjustment to self and to reality; that to consider it a disease merely gives drinkers an excuse to avoid responsibility for their actions in that they cannot be expected to do anything about an illness; that since we are used to thinking of disease in terms of medical cures, this concept will encourage drinkers to think there must a pill or potion that will make it well.

A compromise position of sorts between these two extreme positions holds that the early phase of alcoholism where the person drinks to get high or to relieve some discomfort is symptomatic of some underlying pathology, while at the end of the process when tolerance, physical dependence, loss of control and craving ensues, alcoholism becomes a disease.

Another point of view is that we usually think of disease as involving physical symptoms, but that inasmuch as a large percentage of physical illnesses can have psychogenic roots — addictions having both physical and psychological components — references to addictions as diseases are valid.

Probably the only significance the disease concept will have for the average drinking person is whether treatment for the condition is covered by private insurance or workmens' compensation programs and the viability of certain treatment programs that insist the alcoholic is a sick person.

An early pioneer in the study of alcohol abuse was Dr. E. M. Jellinek, who as a result of various studies involving mostly members of Alcoholics Anonymous established the idea of the inevitable progression of early drinking behavior to eventual alcoholism. Because the studies were based on the reports of men who had mostly progressed into alcoholism over a period of fifteen to twenty years of increasing problem drinking, the progression phenomenon became reinforced as a major characteristic of alcoholism.[12]

The progression concept still enjoys a great deal of popularity, inside and outside AA, in spite of the fact that many subsequent studies from the 1960s until the present have failed to support it. In other words, the old AA saying, "once an alcoholic, always an alcoholic," just "ain't necessarily so."

Later in this work an entire chapter will be devoted to
Alcoholics Anonymous, its origins, its purposes and functions,
its traditions, its strengths and weaknesses, its successes and its
failures.

TRADITIONAL TREATMENT

Supposing you are exhibiting symptoms of extreme problem drinking or alcoholism and want to do something about it, what are your options? Of course you can continue to drink and so suffer the normal consequences of that, and many people choose to do just that if that's what they truly want to do. Others try one or more of the various treatment modalities available, with varying degrees of success. Others, having already made a firm decision to terminate drinking, seek support from some treatment center, which then gets credit for the "cure." And still others simply choose to stop drinking, if that's what they truly want to do.

Briefly here are some of the methods or techniques that have been used over the years in attempts to treat persons exhibiting symptoms of problem drinking or alcoholism. While these methods are described separately they are usually not available in their pure form since most clinicians choose to use a combination of different techniques. They realize the variability of the human mind and the fact that methods that seem to work for one person may not work at all for another and that

27

a combination of methods may be necessary in order to get through to a particular individual, if indeed he can be reached at all. Then, of course, there is great variability in the setting in which these techniques are applied. Separate chapters have been devoted to two modalities that this writer feels are of particular significance in dealing with alcohol abuse, namely Alcoholics Anonymous and Reality Therapy.

PSYCHOANALYSIS is a technique originated by Sigmund Freud, often referred to as the father of human psychology. Basically it deals with the conflict between the conscious and unconscious and recognizes the problems inherent in man's dual nature, as a biological animal and social being. The therapist plays a passive role, encouraging the patient to talk about anything that enters her mind, a process known as "free association." Theoretically, over a period of time the patient and psychiatrist relive the patient's experiences and attitudes, which are then transferred to the psychiatrist who interprets them in such a way that the patient understands the unconscious conflicts that govern her behavior and makes the desired changes.

This procedure is very time consuming, usually quite expensive and of questionable effectiveness in its classical form. Consequently many changes have been made in recent years in order to give it more relevancy to alcoholism. The person interested in pursuing a more detailed discussion of the application of the principles of psychoanalysis specifically to the peculiar problems of alcoholism is referred to *Principles of Alcoholism Psychotherapy*, by Sheldon Zimberg.[13]

BEHAVIOR THERAPY is a technique based on the assumption that alcohol abuse is a socially acquired, learned behavior pattern. It may have its origin in social, psychological or physiological factors or, more likely, in all three. The need for social recognition or peer approval, social ease or spontaneity are significant, as is the need to reduce tension and anxiety.

Physical desire to avoid or postpone withdrawal symptoms like delirium tremens (DTs) may cause drinking behavior to continue.

Behaviorists also believe that what can be learned can be unlearned or relearned and that deficiencies in learning can be corrected by new information. In other words, since people learn to rely on alcohol to ease their pain, reduce tension or put themselves at greater ease socially, they can likewise be taught other means of accomplishing the same ends, means that are not self destructive or damaging to others. Various behavioral treatment approaches have been developed to attempt to modify inappropriate drinking behaviors:

Operant conditioning - Inappropriate drinking behavior is punished by the withholding of privileges or deprivation of something of value to the patient. Rewards for appropriate drinking or abstinence are also used.

Contingency contracting - This has been found effective in a home environment. With this technique the alcoholic signs a contract limiting the permissibly amount of alcohol per day that may be consumed. If this amount is exceeded he or she must forfeit a fine to a significant other.

Aversion therapy - This technique is used experimentally in the study of alcohol abuse and its control, as well as in practice in many alcoholic treatment facilities in the actual treatment of problem drinking, with mixed results. Put in the simplest possible terms, it amounts to conditioning a drinking person to associate some physical, emotional or intellectual discomfort with inappropriate drinking behavior. Different techniques have been devised to accomplish conditioning. They are discussed separately but briefly:

Electrical aversive stimulation **-** With this technique electric shocks are used as the aversive stimulus. This is usually accomplished by pairing mild electric shock with the sight, smell and taste of alcohol, with the hope that once the person becomes conditioned to this association, contact with alcohol will be avoided. The conditioning is accomplished by attaching wires from an electrical shocking device to some point on the person's body, and every time the person sees, smells or tastes alcohol a shock is administered. If this is repeated often enough over a long enough period of time, the conditioning occurs, at least in theory.

Escape conditioning - With this technique the person is given a fairly strong shock when she takes a drink into the mouth, but the shock is terminated when the drink is spit out.

Pseudoconditioning - This involves random-shock techniques where the drinker is sometimes given a strong shock for inappropriate drinking behavior but never knows just when it will be administered. The uncertainty becomes an aversive stimulus on an emotional or intellectual level.

Sham-conditioning - This is another method, in which no shock is actually administered but the client doesn't know that and keeps expecting it. A technique has even been developed whereby the drinking person carries a portable shocking device so that at appropriate times a shock may be self-administered as a deterrent to inappropriate drinking behavior, although it would seem that any person possessing enough willpower to push the button could probably resist the drink without the necessity for an electrical shock.

In a well reasoned review of the history of electrical aversive therapy, G. Terence Wilson, Ph. D., then professor of psychology and co-director of the Alcohol Behavior Research Laboratory at Rutgers University, stated that this method had become the most widely used and intensively researched form of aversion therapy. He concluded, however, that evidence on the effectiveness of the technique is overwhelmingly negative and that its use as a treatment modality with alcoholics should be discontinued. [14]

Chemical aversion conditioning - This method of therapy employs nausea-producing drugs such as emetin and apomorphine as the aversive stimuli. The drinking person is conditioned to associate the nausea produced by these drugs with inappropriate drinking behavior. This is believed to be much more effective than electrical aversive therapy. Wilson considered it promising, although he concluded that tests indicated not all alcoholics are candidates for aversion therapy.[15] Some studies have been done with another chemical that does not induce nausea. Succinylcholine is administered intravenously to induce paralysis and respiratory arrest for a minute or so, reportedly a terrifying experience, as the aversive stimulus.

Symbolic aversive stimulation - Sometimes called *"covert sensitization"*. It involves pairing the actual or imagined smell and taste of alcohol with imagined nausea, hangover, headaches or other aversive imagery, either under hypnosis or after the client has been trained in deep muscular relaxation. It is felt by some researchers to be superior to electrical aversion therapy in that it may be more readily self directed by the drinking person and it is ethically more appealing and more biologically appropriate, but its effectiveness in the reduction of alcohol consumption over a period of time is subject to question. [16]

Remember in your old drinkin' days how you and your buddies
used to sing this old song, or a version of it?

Drunk last night, drunk the night before
Gonna get drunk tonight like I never got drunk before,
'Cuz when I'm drunk I'm happy as can be,
For I am a member of the Souse family.

Now the Souse family is the best family
That ever came over from old Germany.
There's the highland Dutch and the lowland Dutch
The Rotterdam Dutch and the Goddam' Dutch.

Sing glorious, glorious,
One keg of beer for the four of us
Glory be to God that there are no more of us
For one of us could drink it all alone - Dam near!!

. . . .And how you felt the next mornin'. . . .?

ALCOHOLICS ANONYMOUS

Alcoholics Anonymous is a self help organization consisting of many local support groups that offer assistance and guidance to alcohol abusers. Its initials, AA, have become as familiar to Americans over the age of fifteen as FBI or YWCA and almost equally familiar to the rest of the world. So firmly has it become established in our cultural and social milieu, as well as in the medical, psychological and religious literature, that rarely does a treatment modality omit AA from its list of resources. Since its inception, AA's success in releasing alcoholics from the "curse of their disease" has been legendary but, like most legends, AA has its share of half-truths and myths, heroes and dragons, exaggerations and even failures.

If you are a person with a drinking problem or if you are in close contact with a person who has an alcohol related problem you may have been referred to AA a number of times and you may well be wondering just what it's all about. Probably more people are referred to AA than any other alcohol agency, yet many of the persons and agencies doing the referring — doctors, lawyers, judges, ministers, mental health practitioners, counselors and other professionals — have never attended an AA meeting and have only the vaguest notion of the actual workings of the AA program. Even the literature distributed by AA itself does not give a clear picture. Here is how it works.

Originally AA was basically a religious approach to coping with a drinking problem. Early on, AA's founders realized this approach would offend some people so in an effort to soften this effect they attempted to label the AA program as "spiritual" rather than "religious," but if there is a real difference in these terms in this context it is semantic rather than practical, and the genuinely religious nature of the movement will be obvious to the reader a little later on when we get into the roots and early history of AA. Because of these primarily religious origins you will probably get more out of AA if you can achieve a "spiritual or religious experience, a conversion" as anticipated by the founders. But, in the absence of such an experience, you may still benefit from the alcohol-free environment of the meetings and the genuinely warm, friendly, supportive approach to a common problem. And it is free and readily available almost everywhere.

While the author has not found all members of AA to be equally dedicated to its principles, generally speaking an alcohol abuser who sincerely seeks help will be given it, although help is not proffered and must usually be sought. Long drives, foul weather, late hours, and personal inconvenience do not deter dedicated AA members from giving freely of their help, at any time of the day or night. They always remember when they were on the other side of the fence and are always aware that they still have the "disease" and may, themselves, need help again. The rendering of such help is considered a necessary and therapeutic part of the AA program, in accordance with the "twelfth step" as described later.

AA has chapters everywhere, in over 100 countries and in almost every community in the U. S. and Canada. Many cities and communities have more than one chapter, sometimes oriented toward a special group, minority or life style; for example: Spanish American, Native American, gays, veterans, women, lawyers and others. Historically AA meetings have been places of dense cigarette smoke, but there are now smoke-free meetings, so you can find a group into which you can easily fit. The average chapter has people from many social levels, economic levels, educational levels and professions so there is no need to feel out of place. However, the first meeting may cause some apprehension, and for this reason it may be better if you can arrange to attend with a friend or acquaintance. It feels good to sit there in the company of someone you know and trust. If you cannot attend with someone, call AA in advance and ask for someone to pick you up. This is not an imposition, as you will learn later in the program. Part of the therapy of AA is in welcoming and counseling new members or prospective members, so don't feel guilty about asking for help. You will have your chance to return the favor. You will find AA listed in the yellow pages under "Alcoholism."

Most AA meetings are "open,"so you can feel comfortable taking your spouse or significant other, whether or not they have a drinking problem, but you should check first as there are occasional closed meetings. If you can arrive a little early you may be able to meet a few other people, perhaps some of them new, which will also help to put you at ease. And — there is always the coffee pot.

AA meetings, wherever held, tend to be quite similar, perhaps even a bit ritualistic. Usually someone with some experience with AA meetings will have been chosen to "chair" the meeting, which means he or she will open and close the meeting and give the members and guests an opportunity to express themselves if they wish. When the chairperson gets around to you, which probably will happen, you are not required to respond and you will not be criticized if you do not, but it is believed by AA to be therapeutic to share your failures, fears and hopes with the group. If you want to wait until your second or third meeting to respond you may certainly do so.

One thing you will notice is that as each person speaks he or she states approximately as follows: "I'm Jane (or John) and I'm an alcoholic," whereupon everyone in the room responds, "Hi, Jane (or John)", and then the person proceeds to say what he or she has to say. Last names are eliminated in all phases of the AA experience, thus insuring the anonymity that is so important to the organization, and the words "I'm an alcoholic" affirm one of the basic principles of AA, "that we are alcoholic and cannot manage our own lives."

Each person may say whatever is on his mind, but usually it consists of personal experiences and problems with drinking; how sobriety was achieved, if in fact it is believed to have been; religious, spiritual or philosophical insights and testimonials; and hopes for a life of sobriety. There usually is no time limit, much to the chagrin of some of the members of long standing who may have heard a twenty minute story with various embellishments over and over again. These dissertations are often referred to as "drunkalogues" or "horror stories," affectionately or sarcastically, depending on one's point of view, but they are considered by AA to be therapeutic and as such are encouraged. The personal stories are often touching indeed, and this writer has frequently sat through a meeting with a lump in his throat and tears in his eyes.

When the last person has had an opportunity to speak and the chairperson has added his or her own remarks and appropriate announcements, the meeting is adjourned and refreshments served, with emphasis on the ever present coffee pot. Then people just visit, get acquainted, make small talk, counsel each other, share more experiences and generally socialize until ready to go home.

Of course there are a number of variations of the meeting format. Sometimes members will read aloud from the "Big Book" [17] or some other AA approved literature; often guest speakers will address the group on some inspirational or alcohol related topic; films and slides are sometimes shown.

There are some words and cliches that you will frequently hear and with which you should be familiar:

"**Higher Power**" - God, as we understand Him - The term was apparently devised to facilitate AA's desire to be known as a spiritual rather than religious approach, and thus to permit the drinker to identify herself with whatever form of deity her mind could devise, but in any case a power greater than herself.

"**Once an alcoholic, always an alcoholic**" - An inflexible AA concept that alcoholism is a disease that one gets and from which he cannot and will not recover. There is no scientific basis for the universal application of this concept and many studies have so indicated, [18,19] but still AA hangs in there.

"**The alcoholic is sick**" and "**alcoholism is a disease**" - These statements reflect AA's acceptance of the disease concept of alcoholism, that it is a disease rather than a symptom of some underlying emotional or other condition. A more complete discussion of this concept will be found elsewhere in this work.

"**Only an alcoholic can help an alcoholic**" - This idea is frequently expressed by many of the older AA members, that only AA is effective in the treatment of alcoholism, an opinion certainly not shared by any treatment modality and one without any factual basis.

"One day at a time" - This is an AA concept that it is unrealistic to commit one's self to sobriety for more than one day at a time, so each morning one pledges himself to sobriety for the ensuing twenty-four hours.

"Fake it 'till you make it " - Pretend until you can accept.

H.A.L.T. - Don't get too Hungry, Angry, Lonely or Tired.

"Hitting bottom" or **"bottoming out"** - This is the point at which the alcoholic acknowledges dependence upon and powerlessness over alcohol.

"Fifth stepping" - This is listening while an AA member admits the nature of her wrongs, in accordance with the fifth step, described later on.

"Twelfth stepping" - This is helping other AA members achieve sobriety and work the AA program, in accordance with the twelfth step.

A few others that are self explanatory are: "First things first," "easy does it," "live and let live," "keep an open mind," "let go and let God," and "there, but for the grace of God."

So, what does AA do to help you cope with your drinking problem? First, and perhaps by far most important, it provides a supportive, non threatening, alcohol free social environment where you may meet, counsel and share experience with other people with whom you share a common characteristic— you have a disease called alcoholism. You learn that the disease, as such, is incurable and will be with you until death, that the only acceptable way to cope with the disease, since there is no cure, is total abstinence, that total abstinence is not likely to be achieved without the assistance of the AA program but that people who really "work the program" of AA will probably succeed.

"Working the program" consists of following the twelve steps to recovery and observing the twelve AA traditions, all of which are set out in full later in this chapter. Basically it amounts to accepting the fact of alcoholism and your own inability to deal with it, abandoning your own futile attempts to deal with it, and turning it over to "God, as we understand him" (**Higher Power**). Now you can see why it would be helpful if you could enjoy a "spiritual or religious experience — a conversion" somewhere along the way. There are those who claim you can work the program without the necessity for any real spiritual or religious zeal, but this tortured interpretation of the plain, clear language of the twelve steps smacks of an intellectual dishonesty which may partially account for the alcohol abuser's predicament.

A brief history of the development of AA helps one to better understand the nature of its basic philosophy. In 1931 a wealthy young man named Rowland H., having tried every known treatment for his drinking problem, finally went to Europe and sought help from the famous Swiss psychiatrist, Dr. Carl Gustav Jung. After a lengthy attempt at treating Rowland, Dr. Jung gave up but offered him some form of hope, the possibility of a "spiritual or religious experience — in short, a genuine conversion." He cautioned, however, that recovery as a result of such an experience was comparatively rare. Well, it worked. Indirectly word of Rowland's experience got to one William G. Wilson, affectionately (and appropriately anonymously) now known to AA members as Bill W., a co-founder of AA. Bill W. credited Dr. Jung's statement as being the first foundation stone upon which AA was built. [20]

Dr. Robert Smith, referred to in AA literature as Dr. Bob, was the other co-founder of AA. Both he and Bill W., of course, were practicing alcoholics prior to their "conversions." The personal stories of these men are truly touching and may

be read in detail in the **"Big Book."** Biographical sketches of
these men and other persons instrumental in the founding and
early development of AA, as well as a scholarly treatment of the
history of the movement, may be found in *Not God, A History
of Alcoholics Anonymous.* [21]

The founders of AA compiled a list of twelve steps
which they took in order to stop drinking. They recommended
these steps to the AA membership as a program of recovery.
The steps are set out here in full, along with some of the material
that introduces them in the **Big Book**: "Remember that we deal
with alcohol - cunning, baffling, powerful! Without help it is
too much for us. But there is One who has all power - that One
is God. May you find Him now! Half measures availed us
nothing. We stood at the turning point. We asked His protection and care with complete abandon. Here are the steps we
took, which are suggested as a program of recovery:

1. We admitted we were powerless over alcohol - that
our lives had become unmanageable.

2. Came to believe that a Power greater than ourselves
could restore us to sanity.

3. Made a decision to turn our will and our lives over
to the care of <u>God as we understood Him</u>.

4. Made a searching and fearless moral inventory of
ourselves.

5. Admitted to God, to ourselves, and to another human
being the exact nature of our wrong.

6. Were entirely ready to have God remove all these
defects of character.

7. Humbly asked Him to remove our shortcomings.

8. Made a list of all persons we had harmed, and
became willing to make amends to them all.

9.   Made direct amends to such people wherever possible, except when to do so would injure them or others.

10. Continued to take personal inventory and when we were wrong promptly admitted it.

11. Sought through prayer and meditation to improve our conscious contact with God <u>as we understood Him</u>, praying only for knowledge of His will for us and the power to carry that out.

12. Having had a spiritual awakening as a result of these steps, we tried to carry this message to alcoholics, and to practice these principles in all our affairs." [22]

After listing the twelve steps, the writers of the **Big Book** then listed, apparently as general policy, "....three pertinent ideas:

(a) That we were alcoholic and could not manage our own lives.

(b) That probably no human power could have relieved our alcoholism.

(c) That God could and would if He were sought." [23]

A chapter "We Agnostics" was included in the **Big Book**. The message of this chapter is that alcoholic agnostics and atheists are handicapped by obstinacy, sensitiveness and unreasoning prejudice, so touchy that even casual references to spiritual things make them bristle with antagonism. They must abandon this type of thinking and open their minds to the existence of a Higher Power or be doomed to an alcoholic death. "To be doomed to an alcoholic death or to live on a spiritual basis are not always easy alternatives to face...." [24] but according to the **Big Book** they are the <u>only</u> alternatives.

While the position of AA is thus clearly stated, in practice this strict approach is considerably softened. It has been said that even Bill W. and Dr. Bob publicly played down their religious beliefs to encourage a wider membership. [25]   It is not unusual to hear AA members state their understanding that they need not subscribe to the religious and spiritual requirements of the **Big Book** in any literal sense. One enthusiastic member proclaimed her right to adopt a light bulb as her Higher Power if she chose, though I seriously doubt that's what Bill W. and Dr. Bob had in mind. But perhaps it serves to point out the fact that with or without a Higher Power an alcohol abuser can gain great strength and determination from the many other facets of the AA fellowship. In many localities AA may be the only facility available to the alcohol abuser, so he would be well advised to accept the parts of the program he can use and either reject or minimize the rest. This may put him somewhat in conflict with certain administrators of AA oriented programs since "working the program" is often given a literal interpretation, particularly by the old timers.

In answer to the self directed questions, "How can AA best function?" and, "How can AA best stay whole and so survive?", AA has presented its **twelve traditions**, set out here in their short form:

1. Our common welfare should come first; personal recovery depends on AA unity.

2. For our group purpose there is but one ultimate authority — a loving God as He may express Himself in our group conscience. Our leaders are but trusted servants; they do not govern.

3. The only requirement for AA membership is a desire to stop drinking.

4. Each group should be autonomous except in matters affecting other groups or AA as a whole.

5. Each group has but one primary purpose — to carry its message to the alcoholic who still suffers.

6. An AA group ought never endorse, finance or lend the AA name to any related facility or outside enterprise, lest

problems of money, property and prestige divert us from our primary purpose.

7.   Every AA group ought to be self supporting, declining outside contributions.

8. Alcoholics Anonymous should remain forever non-professional, but our service centers may employ special workers.

9. AA, as such, ought never be organized; but we may create service boards or committees directly responsible to those they serve.

10. Alcoholics Anonymous has no opinion on outside issues; hence the AA name ought never be drawn into public controversy.

11. Our public relations policy is based on attraction rather than promotion; we need always maintain personal anonymity at the level of press, radio and films.

12. Anonymity is the spiritual foundation of all our traditions, ever reminding us to place principles before personalities.[26]

Most of these have to do with AA's existence as an organization rather than with the individual member trying to achieve sobriety.

Although AA has historically preferred to call itself a spiritual program rather than a religious one, it has been described by at least one student of comparative religions as a "typically American religious phenomenon" with "Evangelical, Pietist insight." [27]   Whatever view one might adopt, it seems clear from reading the history of the movement that the basic precepts of AA, the twelve traditions, the twelve steps and other doctrinal matters were hardly divinely inspired. Rather they evolved out of compromise, personality clashes, internal and external politics, financial constraints, philosophical differences, in-fighting between two major camps and other typically human considerations. The reader inter-

ested in pursuing this evolutionary process in detail is referred
again to *Not God, A History of Alcoholics Anonymous.* [28]

Extravagant claims for the many successes of AA in
enabling "countless" problem drinkers to achieve sobriety
abound in the alcohol studies literature.[29] Strangely lacking is
the presence of any meaningful data to support these claims. A
request for success data directed to the General Service Board
of Alcoholics Anonymous, Inc. produced a survey purporting
to show the total membership of AA in the U. S. and Canada and
little else. One author, in addressing the question of AA's
effectiveness, states: "The AA contention that it is the most
effective method, if not the only one, does serve to enhance the
morale of its actual and potential members. Useful as this
propaganda is in helping alcoholics to accept AA, it should not
be overestimated at the expense of other facilities and treatment
modalities that make fewer claims but attempt to validate those
they do make."[30] In fairness it must be noted that validation of
claims to success is rare throughout the field of alcohol treatment.

AA works for some people, it does not work for others.
One of my dearest friends, Bill F., is seventy-two years of age,
a wirey, active outgoing man who has been alcohol free for
some thirty-four years. He credits AA with his sobriety and
enthusiastically supports the principals of that organization. He
has devoted a good part of the last thirty-four years to attempting to help other alcoholics achieve and maintain sobriety
within the framework of AA.

Bill was born in a sod shack on the Montana prairies
without the aid of a doctor. He reports that his childhood was
so unhappy that at the age of eleven he left the house with a rifle,
intending to take his own life. But being a Catholic he realized
this was an "unforgivable act," since he would not be alive to
ask forgiveness so he changed his mind.

There was always "home brew" beer in the cellar and a

still was operated on the farm before prohibition ended, so Bill believes he started drinking at about the age of thirteen. On his first binge he ended up in a slough on the ranch, wet, cold and sick. Not long after that he attended a dance, and two of his brothers' girl friends tried to drag him onto the dance floor. He was paralyzed with fear and broke away from them to find his brother's car and drink some of his whiskey. This softened his fear somewhat and he returned to the dance.

In 1940 Bill graduated from high school, then lived the life of a cowboy, getting drunk in town frequently, not trusting anyone who didn't drink, passing out from overindulgence and being brought home by other ranch hands. He was first arrested in 1953, for hit-and-run, then later arrested for being drunk when found lying in the street after having been severly beaten and thrown out of a car. On another occasion he was beaten almost to death but rushed to the hospital. When he had been treated he became so violent they had to lock him up.

Bill married at twenty-three, but the marriage soon failed. He then tried to kill his former wife's lover with a rifle, failed, then tried to beat him to death the next day. No charges were ever filed. He set his house on fire when falling into a drunken stupor, but the fire went out or he would surely have died of smoke inhalation.

At twenty-six Bill moved to Oregon, tried the mobile home business, then the building business. Alcohol was always a part of his life. Both businesses failed.

Asked how he happened to quit drinking, Bill replied, "My surrender came at a religious retreat. I felt I had no choice but to try, a day at a time. Working for my board, finding a carpenter job and an old trailer to live in, making AA meetings and total abstinence. I made sixty days sober — the first time in twenty years. I made the child support payments and no more jails. The desire to see the children I had abandoned grew.

Sober 120 days I stopped in front of my old home and three beautiful children ran out and loved the old alcoholic— my first real acceptance. After a couple of years of sobriety I had some business successes and I controlled over a million dollars worth of property. My children moved in with me. But I went broke again and I went to work as a farm hand to support the four of us.

"For the first six years without alcohol I went through a lot of problems with my kids. The two teen-aged boys were getting into trouble drinking and I feared for my teen aged daughter, but I trusted the recovering alcoholics that always seemed to be a part of my life. Then one night I was bullied into attending a party and was to take a young widow. I expected the usual rejection and was amazed to be accepted instead and to have her accept my family as well. She was very beautiful, and ten days later I asked her to be my wife and she accepted."

Bill is still married to this wonderful lady, but life has been anything but easy. One son was killed in an automobile accident when he was drunk. The other son and his daughter are practicing alcoholics. Money has been an ongoing problem. But through it all he has managed to maintain his sobriety. "I still go to two AA meetings a week," he reports, "To be sober physically, mentally, emotionally and spiritually, to the best of my ability today, I need my fellow persons who understand what it is like to stand one drink away from total destruction." AA has worked for Bill.

But contrast Bill's story with that of Eric. At the time I knew him Eric was a friendly, cooperative, middle aged, single man living in a residential recovery unit stressing AA as its primary treatment focus. At the age of fourteen he stole a bottle of wine to see what it would be like to drink alcohol. He got drunk and liked it. After that he would steal drinks from his father's whiskey bottle, refilling it with water. At sixteen he married a girl he had impregnated.

At nineteen Eric had been divorced and was back living with his mother, who would buy liquor for him since he was yet under age. He reports she had no objection to his drinking, even though he frequently drank until he passed out. He managed to finish high school and a year of junior college before going to work. He completed a plastering apprenticeship and an electrical apprenticeship but eventually got a job as a tire repairman and worked his way up to store manager. Alcohol was a constant companion.

By the age of thirty-one drinking had caused drastic physical problems. "I had my spleen removed and an arterial by-pass done on my heart, had seventy-three blood transfusions, was in the hospital for seventy-three days in intensive care and they told me that if ever I drank again I would surely die. Three days from the day they released me from the hospital I fell down on the ice due to being intoxicated. I busted open all the incisions and had to go back into the hospital and the doctor told me I was absolutely nuts. But one thing it did do, I didn't drink on a day to day basis any more. I became a periodical drunk. I would heal up enough to get well — back on my feet — and go on a binge, drinking all the way from twelve to twenty-five days at a shot and get sick enough to where I'd just about have to be carted away in an ambulance or I'd end up in detox.

"Between 1971 and 1982, when I first got to this agency where I am now, I had already went through three and a half years incarcerated, behind bars on different occasions, for driving under the influence — no violent crimes, no wrecks, no manslaughters — things like this. It was all due to just driving and drinking. I had been through eleven different treatment programs by the time I got here. Everything from the Gresham Care Unit, right on through the state hospital programs, an all-Indian program where I was the only white man in the whole group. I went into that to see if I could be accepted. I used them.

I became a treatment junkie, is what I became.

"Raleigh Hills wouldn't take me. But I did go for out-patient hypnosis therapy and that didn't take. I feel at this time in my life as I look back, I think that a lot of those programs would have worked if I had used them the way they were designed. But I got pretty good as a professional. I could talk the jargon and I could walk the walk and come in sick and disgusted and be voted most likely to succeed, but most of the programs knew me as I was throughout the state and wouldn't let me back in anymore. So I finally decided that I had one other alternative — that I needed to find a program that would give me enough time to really work on myself. I heard about this agency and I came down here and was in treatment for a seven month period and then stayed on as a counselor in training. I managed to accumulate almost seven years before going back out."

Asked why he happened to leave the facility he replied, "I, ah, got away from my program, had a lot of resentments I wasn't dealing with. I, ah, went through a divorce a year and a half prior to going out, felt a lot of resentment in that one particular area, I lost contact with my, ah, my God of my understanding. I wasn't praying and meditating as I normally used to do and I thought that if I could help all these other people here in treatment that my program really didn't need all that much work. Y'know, I thought I was just about ready to walk on water, which was far from the case.

"I went out and got drunk and that was grounds for discharge. And I understood that when I went to town. My old patterns came right back to me, flashed across to me. One day I wasn't in a bad mood, I wasn't in a depressed state, I just decided to heck with it — I'm through. I'm gonna go get drunk. I need to blank it all out for a while, and I knew how I could do it and I did it. I made the decision to get drunk. Nobody bent my elbow. I made the decision."

For two and a half years Eric engaged in binge drinking, each binge resulting in eventual hospitalization. He described his present physical problems : "Heart palpitations, pains in my chest, having trouble getting my breath, DT's, severe shakes, and all the time this was going on my neurological problems in my feet were getting worse and worse and worse and my feet are now numb due to my alcoholism. I have a right leg that's numb above the knee and I also have recently had a colostomy. The colostomy was not the fault of alcoholism, however. I can finally say I went to the hospital when it wasn't my alcoholism (laughing)."

Eric has been through many treatment programs, including Gestalt, Rational Emotive Therapy and many others he can't remember. He feels he learned a lot but just wasn't ready to quit drinking. He is now afraid that if he does take another drink it will kill him. Asked if he would at this point be willing to make a commitment not to ever drink again he replied, "I can't say for sure at this point that I would never take another drink. I doubt if I'll ever be able to do so. Right now I'm comfortable with one day at a time. I can live one day at a time — I don't like to project. . ." He admits that leaves tomorrow open for drinking.

"I start every day off with, ah, a prayer to my Higher Power that He will be with me and guide and direct me in every way possible and keep me in a position where I abstain from alcohol and due to the spiritual growth that I've seen and the commitment I've made to the God that I understand. I leave my life in His hands, more or less, and with Him being by my side I feel that, ah, my recovery is more or less, ah, in a lot more positive position than it ever has in my life."

I mentioned I had noticed that a great many people who have been exposed to the "one day at a time" concept prevalent in AA have trouble conceiving of ever making a commitment for a **life of sobriety** — only for a day. He replied, "Oh, I make a commitment for a life of sobriety, but only for a day at a time. I suppose there's an inconsistency there, but it works for me."

Has AA worked for Eric? The last time I heard of him he was actively drinking again, though he knows it will undoubtedly kill him.

What does this author think of AA? I believe that AA is a valuable tool for getting a serious alcohol abuser sober and started on the road to finding new and better ways of meeting his needs. Often it is the only mechanism for accomplishing that, particularly for indigent people. It is free and it is everywhere. But unfortunately it often encourages the alcoholic to remain in that stage rather than moving on to take control of his life. It becomes almost a cult which is difficult to leave and from which he is not encouraged to depart. It is hoped that eventually this worthwhile organization will evolve to the point that it encourages people to make a commitment to permanent sobriety, not just for a day at a time, then get on with their lives — **Beyond AA**.

REALITY THERAPY and CONTROL THEORY

Upon my retirement from the practice of law it became possible to return to studies related to alcohol abuse. My first effort was directed at reviewing all the psychological concepts studied in my undergraduate days in the hope of finding a method that might show promise for the alcoholic. Very little was found. Most involved probing into the abuser's mind, his past, conscious, unconscious, subconscious, in a search for the reasons for the drinking behavior, and/or doing something to or for the drinker to cause him to change. The alcoholic was almost universally considered a victim of outside forces over which he really had no conscious control.

Then I ran across a book that had been published after my undergraduate days, *Reality Therapy* by William Glasser,[31] that seemed to offer what I had been seeking. I called Dr. Glasser in Los Angeles to tell him of my appreciation of his work and was surprised to learn that he personally was conducting classes and a seminar commencing the following week and that I was invited to attend. Of course I accepted.

One of the factors that so appealed to me in Glasserian psychology was that it completely divorced itself from the, until then, standard approaches to psychological analysis and treatment, which I had learned had not worked very well, particularly for persons with substance abuse problems. As Glasser points out, conventional psychiatry followed these principles:

(1) That mental illness can be classified, and can be treated according to these diagnostic classifications.

(2) That an essential part of therapy is probing in the patient's past life since once he understands the roots of his problem he can change his attitude about life and develop more effective living patterns.

(3) That if the patient will transfer his attitudes toward people to the therapist, the therapist can relive experiences with the patient and the patient, through the therapist's interpretation of this "transference" behavior, will gain insight into his past, thereby enabling him to give up old attitudes and solve his problem.

(4) Unconscious mental conflicts are more important than conscious problems and the patient must be made aware of them through interpretation of dreams, transference and "free associations."

(5) Deviant behavior is considered a product of mental illness and the patient should not be held morally responsible because he is helpless to do anything about it.

(6) Teaching better behaviors is not important since the patient will learn better behaviors himself once he understands the historical and unconscious sources of his problems.[32]

Glasser believes in a much closer involvement with the patient than is usually achieved in conventional treatment; therefore, he challenges each of the foregoing concepts as follows:

(1)   The concept of mental illness is unacceptable since the patient cannot become really involved with us as a mentally ill person who is not accountable for his behavior.

(2) Since we cannot change a patient's past nor accept the fact that he is limited by it we do not delve into the past but concentrate on the present and future.[*]

(3) We relate to patients as fellow humans, not as transference figures.

(4) Since a patient cannot become involved with us by excusing his behavior on the basis of his unconscious motivations we do not look for unconscious conflicts or the reasons for them.

(5)   We face the issue of right and wrong and emphasize the morality of behavior.

(6) We teach patients better ways to fulfill their needs.[33]

Reduced to its simplest possible terms, Glasser's concept is that man's ultimate goal is to satisfy his basic needs and that all pathological behaviors from overindulgence in food or drink to disorders of the mind involving complete loss of contact with reality are simply ineffective and many times irresponsible efforts to satisfy those basic needs. Although such behaviors may seem to us to be obviously inappropriate, they are the best the person can come up with at the time and under his or her circumstances, but it is quite possible for the person to be taught more appropriate, responsible behaviors, and that is the function of Reality Therapy.

---

[*] As this is written a furious debate is raging within the psychological community over the nature of memories, their accuracy and reliability, their suppression and subsequent recovery, their admission as evidence in court and ethical and legal implications involved in memory recovery methods, particularly memories of child sexual abuse, satanic ritual abuse, past life regression and experiences with aliens from outer space.

In order to fulfill the basic needs we must be involved with at least one other person, and preferably more than one. We cannot fulfill our needs without **at least one person who cares for us and for whom we care**, and this person or persons must be in touch with reality and able to fulfill his or her own needs. In the original work, *Reality Therapy*, Dr. Glasser described two basic needs: the need to love and be loved and the need to feel that we are worthwhile to ourselves and others. In his subsequent book, *Control Theory,*[34] he has revised the list of basic needs to include the following which, of course, were implied in the earlier version:

(1) **The need to survive and reproduce.**

The human brain consists of two major sections, a tiny part at the very top of the spinal column that Glasser refers to as the old brain, since it probably evolved first in early man, and the new brain, which evolved much later and is much larger. The old brain controls our automatic body functions such as sexual urges, heartbeat, breathing, digestion, blood pressure and immune system and has a great deal to do with our need, and ability, to survive and reproduce. But while the old brain has ways of letting us know when one or more of these functions is not operating properly, it usually requires some action on the part of the new brain to do something about it.

If we are suddenly unable to breathe properly the old brain sends a message that we are suffocating and the new brain signals us to immediately get our head above water or quickly grab that inhaler that we've learned will relieve the congestion in our bronchial tubes and permit normal breathing. If our old brain tells us we have not had sex for a long time the new brain begins to look for a sexual outlet of some sort to cure that deficiency, be it sexual intercourse with another person or mere masturbation. Either way, once orgasm occurs the old brain is perfectly satisfied and for a time will not be capable of being overruled by the new brain. The old brain's original purpose was undoubtedly to cause the impregnation of a female human in order to propagate the human species but it has been fooled many times since.

When the old brain signals that our stomach is empty and we need food to keep our body alive our new brain enables us to seek sustenance. Unfortunately the new brain often so enjoys partaking of the sustenance that it ignores the old brain's messages that it has had enough and we keep eating for the sheer pleasure of it. This often results in obesity that then plays havoc with the heart and digestive system, sometimes thus necessitating the old brain's having to send a message that we are having a heart attack, whereupon the new brain tells us to immediately dial 911.

With the exception of breathing, most of the old brain's functions can be frustrated by the new brain's manipulations. If you hold your breath until you reach unconsciousness your old brain automatically kicks in and you begin to breathe again. Those who practice yoga claim to be able to change the rate of heartbeat. Some people choose to remain sexually abstinent for spiritual or metaphysical reasons, although even they may experience spontaneous orgasms during sleep. And if you should choose to "chug" a fifth of whiskey, or consume certain combinations of depressive drugs you can easily shut down the entire system, whereupon you will receive honorable mention in the obituary column and your heirs will begin dividing your assets.

Most of the elements needed to satisfy our need for survival and reproduction consist of **things**. The remaining four needs are psychological and are satisfied more by other people than by things.

(2) **The need to belong — to love, share and cooperate.**

While the need for survival seems to be the most important because food, water, air and good physical health seem so urgent, they only insure continued life. But the quality of that life usually depends upon feelings of genuine belonging — of being of importance to some other human being, of feeling of importance to one's self, of being able receive love in return, of shareing and cooperating with fellow humans. Those who choose to terminate their life usually do so because they are lonely and the quality of their life makes it not worthwhile to continue.

(3) **The need for power.**

Most forms of animal life other than human have very little need for power beyond that required for mating, self-preservation and protection of territory, although the author's farm experience has at times indicated that certain animals use power for the sake of pure orneriness. Only humans seem to require power for its own sake. As Glasser states, only we have a need for getting to the top that keeps us competing long past the time when any rational use exists for this much power or recognition.

The desire for power often conflicts with our need for love and belonging, and we have situations where a couple's loving marriage deteriorates when they reach an irreconcilable struggle for power. Women's pursuit for power used to be hidden but is now noticeably open and aggressive. That is appropriate since a woman's need for power is as great as that of a man, but the woman's departure from a traditional housewife role to secure a college degree in her search for power often conflicts with the husband's traditional ideas of family life and great strife ensues.

Far too often men and women in their unremitting

search for power, find themselves locked into traditional cocktail parties and cocaine parties, seeking to belong to the right groups, to impress the right people and obtain influence, only to discover an addiction they didn't expect and from which they cannot easily recover. Often it is perceived as a part of the effort to juggle the need for belonging with the quest for power.

(4) **The need for freedom.**

Most of us try to avoid jail if for no other reason than the fact that jails deprive us of our freedom to move about as we please. We can, in jail, move about within certain limits but only under the direction of the jailers. We eat what is set before us with no freedom of choice and visit with our loved ones where, when and if the jailer chooses. Perhaps it is because our need for freedom is so powerful that incarceration is one of the oldest forms of punishment known to man. What we seem to want is the freedom to choose how we are to live our lives, to express ourselves freely, to associate with whom we choose, to read and write what satisfies us and to worship or not worship as we wish and believe. Wars have been fought for the sake of these freedoms.

But as with all our needs, the need for freedom often conflicts with our other needs, and rarely do we figure out how to live so that we fulfill all of them to the extent we would like. When we do we are ecstatic since we are, for usually a very short period of time, very much in control of our lives.

(5) **The need for fun.**

Fun, like beauty, is in the eyes of the beholder. I see a news program on television showing thousands of young people twisting and turning to the sounds of music in some huge stadium and I find it difficult to relate to this activity as fun, although the participants are laughing and obviously enjoying themselves. On the other hand I go into my garden and spend a warm spring day planting, cultivating, watering, watching things grow and having great fun in the process, an activity I imagine most of the young people in the news item would find to be hard work and less than enjoyable.

As Glasser points out, laughter is a unique human behavior and he believes that it means we experience a powerful sense that our need for fun has been fulfilled at the moment.

We have more fun with other people than merely by ourselves, since we learn from them. Unfortunately we sometimes learn things we would be better off not knowing. Drinking and drugging activities are examples. Probably no one discovers alcohol or other drugs by himself. Most succumb to peer pressures while very young and agree to "try, just once" a cigarette, a beer. The first cigarette may make a novice cough, even get a bit nauseous, but his need to belong will soon overcome that and he will be puffing away alongside his friends, addicting himself to the most addictive of all drugs, nicotine. The first beer is just a single step up from a can of pop and leaves a slight feeling of well being. It's fun. Illegal purchases soon follow, and gradual escalation to whiskey or vodka often occurs.

Too many people consider alcohol their main source of fun. In moderation it can remain fun for many years, but some eventually find it can cease to be fun and eventually become life's greatest burden.

The author gave up alcohol thirty-six years ago, but still new friends seem mystified and sometimes offended at his refusal to join them in drinking. Alcohol causes many conflicts between various human needs. Frequently the most difficult barrier in crossing from alcohol abuse to sobriety is the surrender of one's drinking cohorts, but a balancing of priorities requires that one seeking sobriety acquire new, non-drinking friends — sometimes not an easy task and often one the person is not willing to face.

Glasser believes that fun is part of life's learning process and that humans never stop learning and having fun doing so, that it is necessary to resolving the conflicts between various needs and their fulfillment. Our continuing struggle to satisfy these disparate forces, and especially to resolve the ever present conflicts between them, has pushed us to become the most intelligent of all living creatures. Driven by our genes we are unable to escape these conflicts. As long as we believe that we are controlled by outside forces we will be unable to solve them. We must accept the fact that all we do, all our behaviors, are our efforts to solve these conflicts by the best means that occur to us at the time. We make errors, but in so doing we can learn more effective methods.

Dr. Glasser is fond of using metaphors to illustrate his explanations of the workings of the human mind. One of the most effective is to imagine all the things we require to fulfill our basic needs to be pictures in our heads, our personal picture album. We store in our personal picture album the pictures of anything in the world that we believe will satisfy one or more of our basic needs. It is not the same as memory, for we have many things in our memory that are not need satisfying although some of them may come in handy in securing things that are need satisfying. When a picture that has been in my album for many years is no longer satisfying as I would like it to be, I will look for a new, more satisfying picture to replace it. This is a metaphorical expression of exactly what happened to me when thirty-six years ago I stopped drinking alcohol. Until then I had for years had this wonderful bottle of whiskey in my picture album, **on page one**, believe me.

When on February 1, 1959, I sat in my office after having my morning vodka, as described in the Preface to this book, I removed that picture from my album and replaced it with a dozen others: a picture of me out of debt and professionally respected (**belonging** and **power**); spending more time with my children (**loving** and **being loved**); sharing more of my time and money with my family (**sharing, cooperating**); doing interesting things with the family and neighbors (**fun**); returning my body to a healthy state (**survival**); being no longer tied to that bottle for relaxation and momentary pleasure (**freedom**). Do you see how dramatically the new outweigh the old? Don't you wonder why so many people fail to recognize this disparity in their personal picture albums before they lose their family, their home, their profession, the respect of their peers? As Dr. Glasser writes, "None of us has a picture in his album of himself doing badly. We may at times choose to do what those around us say is self-destructive, but we don't do these things to destroy ourselves. The pictures we are trying to satisfy make sense to us at the time." One of my drinking companions once held up a pint bottle of whiskey and in all sincerity proclaimed, "You know, Slim, anybody that doesn't drink this stuff has gotta be crazy."

To some the picture of that bottle, or a packet of white powder remains firmly glued in their album, sometimes to be loosened by a heart attack or some other dramatic and threatening occurrence but often remaining throughout their life. And the problem of addiction is no respecter of age, gender, intellect, profession, race, color or social status. Yet, given the proper incentive, and perhaps the knowledge that the pictures can be changed, there is hope for many addicts. That is the function of Reality Therapy and Control Theory.

OUR CONTROL SYSTEM

Everything we do is a behavior, **including our thoughts and feelings**. It is a common misconception about the human brain that our behavior is caused by things that happen to us from the outside. You may have heard in your school days of the scientist named Pavlov who rang a bell each time he fed his dog and claimed that after doing so for a long period of time found that the dog would salivate when the bell was rung, even if the food was not provided. His conclusion was that the **response** of salivating had been **conditioned** by the ringing of the bell.

This was one of the origins of the psychological concept, "conditioned response" that, of course, is the philosophy behind many behavioral approaches to alcohol treatment. Those who adhere to that school of thought feel that if a person is subjected for a long enough period to a painful stimulus when he or she drinks inappropriately, the response will be to give up alcohol (negative reinforcement); or that if the person

61

is rewarded sufficiently for appropriate conduct she will begin
to behave appropriately (positive reinforcement). Many of
these techniques are described in Chapter Four, the infliction of
electric shocks or the administering of chemicals that cause
severe nausea constituting the "stimulus," with the assumption
that the alcohol abuser will "respond" by forever losing her
desire to drink.

The problem with stimulus-response theory is that people
do not always respond to the stimulus as they theoretically
should, just as Pavlov's dog probably didn't always salivate
when the bell was rung. People make choices in their behaviors;
they may or may not respond predictably to a given stimulus.

My uncle, for many years a confirmed alcoholic, was
once mandated by a court to undergo chemical aversion therapy
and he complied. He laughingly stated later that it took him a
week before he was able to get a drink to "ride" (stay down)
but he finally succeeded. His response to the stimulus lasted
less than a week. It wasn't what **he** wanted to do and he
wasn't about to do what someone else wanted him to do.
Quitting drinking was not in his picture album. Subse-
quently he developed emphysema and was told by his physician that he would die if he didn't quit drinking, whereupon
he gave it up without much effort. The picture of continued
life became more important than the picture of the bottle. He
chose to respond positively to the stimulus of the doctor's
advice because he decided he wanted to live. The point is
that while we may be influenced somewhat by outside
factors we **choose our behaviors** and do not simply react or
respond, and we usually don't do something someone else
wants us to do unless it coincides with what we have in our
personal picture album.

From the time we are born (and perhaps even before)
every bit of information we perceive, consciously or otherwise, by means of our sensory organs — sight, hearing, taste,

smell and feel — is stored in our brain and at least theoretically subject to recall when needed. Most of us, when we are
first thrust into a relatively cold and alien world from our
mother's warm and comfortable womb, let our presence be
known by crying. Perhaps this is a random, genetically
programmed reaction to our first transition from one environment to another, but in any case the crying usually gets
someone's attention and our body is wrapped in something
warm. Our mouth is pressed to a warm nipple from which
our innate sucking response enables us to produce a flow of
tasty fluid that curiously solves another problem: that vague
discomfort in our belly we will eventually identify as hun-
ger. At this point, although our brain has not as yet accumulated enough facts to allow us to actually analyze what is
going on, we have stored in our brain some data that will be
subject to recall as needed: crying makes things happen; it
produces warmth and an opportunity to suck; and sucking
eases the discomfort in our belly.

From this moment on, when our sensory organs tell us
we are cold, or our belly feels uncomfortable, we have information in the brain to match up with this sensory input and give us
some idea what to do about it: cry. But now the crying behavior,
rather than being merely random, genetically programmed
behavior, has become a learned, purposeful behavior, a conscious way of exercising control over our life.

From this simple beginning, over the ensuing years the
accumulation of information in the brain grows dramatically in
almost all people. However, since each new item is received,
analyzed and stored by each person's brain in light of, and in
addition to, all previously stored information, and since this
previously stored information is different in each brain, it
follows that what each of us perceives is somehow different
from what every other person perceives. This is true even
though the actual thing, event or condition that gave rise to the

perception was identical.

Since each person views the world differently by reason of his or her personal storehouse of knowledge it is sometimes helpful to consider what each individual knows of the world, as colored by previous perceptions accumulated over the years in the brain, as arranged and rearranged by the ability to reason, and as added to by the ability to invent, to fantasize, to ponder, as being his or her "personal world." Each person has one, and is the center of it, but each person also has an outside world, and all one knows of this outside world is what is perceived by the senses. Unfortunately when we get into an argument or disagreement each of us tends to believe that our personal world is the "real world" which, indeed, it is not. It is only our perception of the real world. We will never really know the real world as such — only what we individually perceive of it.

Although every conscious perception from birth to death becomes a potential part of the brain's storehouse of useful data, there is unfortunately little uniformity or consistency in these data from person to person. One year-old girl has learned that crying results in her being held, fed and loved, with her diaper changed for good measure. Another has learned that crying results in her getting her bottom paddled. Yet another learns that upon crying she is usually left alone for long periods in a cold, dark room. Perhaps another learns that crying produces one result one day and quite another result the following day. Each child is storing different crying data in her brain and each child's future perceptions will be somehow influenced by that difference. When we multiply this simple example by the many thousands of sensory perceptions that each person experiences over the years, the potential for differences among individuals becomes staggering by the time they reach maturity. Thus we are unique; each of us is different from all others; each of us is, truly, one of a kind.

While each of us lives in two worlds, the "outside" world and our own "personal" world, unfortunately the two do not often coincide and we begin to wish our personal world contained more things we observe in the outside world. We attempt to **control** the outside world to fit with our personal world and often it just doesn't work. Another way of putting it is that many of the things we want don't seem to be forthcoming and this result leaves us with pain or discomfort. The difference between what we want or expect and what we get Glasser refers to as an "error," not in the sense of a mistake but as in perception. We attempt to control the outside world in our effort to create the perception that it conforms to our personal world, which, if successful, reduces our "error" to a minimum. In control theory terms we constantly strive to fulfill the pictures in our personal picture album, to do and achieve the things that meet our basic needs.

Usually our efforts to control the outside world involve attempts to control other people. As much as we like to think we are able to control others, we cannot do it unless we somehow persuade them that what we do satisfies some picture in their heads. It is almost impossible to get people to do willingly what does not satisfy some need they have. All these persons have control systems of their own and no one likes to be controlled. Most of us resent others' efforts to control us and we often are angered as a result. A good example of this principle is the preference of many of us to be in our own business rather than work for someone else, even though we may earn far less money and work harder for more hours each day.

Control is not a need but a way we must function to fulfill our needs, and since we all share this characteristic we are engaged in a never ending struggle with each other. But we need each other, so are willing to accept some control — but not too much.

While we have little control over other persons we always have some control over what we ourselves do. But in order to be effective we have to know what is going on inside us and around us. Our five senses, touch, taste, smell, vision and hearing keep us advised as to outside activities and conditions, and we have internal sensors that tell us what is going on inside us, as when we are hungry, tired, thirsty and so on. As previously noted, when we sense that what we have is not what we want, we generate **behaviors** to attempt to remedy that situation. Our total behavior Glasser divides into four separate components: (1) **Doing**, or active behaviors; (2) **Thinking**, the generation of thoughts; (3) **Feeling**, such as anger or joy; and (4) **Physiology**, the generation of voluntary and involuntary body mechanisms like sweating, clenching our fists or gritting our teeth.

To illustrate, imagine that last week I applied for membership in the most prestigious club in town, the Muskrats. All my friends belong; it is acknowledged to be the route to a step up in the local business world in which I am involved. Facilities are available in the club for tennis, golf, exercise, swimming and a host of family activities. My wife and kids are really counting on it. My best friend has recommended me and he is well liked, which makes my acceptance virtually certain. Now, I've just received a note to the effect that I have been refused membership. Somebody on the membership committee has blackballed me.

What I might immediately *do* is to slump down in my chair, avoid my family and friends and wish I had a good stiff drink of whiskey or maybe even take a good drink or two if it is available. My first *thoughts* might be that there must be some mistake, that maybe my application wasn't complete or that I had forgotten to enclose the membership fee with my application, things that would tend to explain or rationalize what happened. My *feelings* would probably include resentment, disappointment, anger, frustration, maybe depression. I might develop a headache, which, together with the components of doing, thinking and feeling constitute my total behavior. I would probably be most aware of one component, disappointment or depression, and if anyone were to ask me how I reacted I'd say "I'm depressed" or "I'm disappointed," for the moment being relatively unaware of the other components of my total behavior. But the more we can learn to recognize that the *feeling* component is only one of the four components of total behavior the more control we will have over our lives.

Within the meaning of Glasser's Control Theory, since feelings are part of total behavior, we have some control over them as we do over all our behaviors. Therefore we cannot consider that feelings happen to us; rather we generate them ourselves. Just as I chose to slump down in my chair and have a couple of shots of whiskey and chose to think of reasons my application had been denied, so, instead of my somehow "being depressed," which presupposes an outside cause, more accurately I "chose to depress," or "chose to anger" as part of my total behavior.

Now, you might try to cheer me up by saying to me, "Well now, this isn't the end of the world. There's still the Moose Lodge and the Eagles Lodge, and besides the Muskrats are a bunch of snobs that you probably wouldn't have liked much anyway. So cheer up." Unfortunately for this effort, if I choose to continue sitting there drinking whiskey, I will not choose to change what I *feel*, for depressing makes good sense to me now and seems to be the best possible choice at the moment. I feel locked into the misery I am experiencing at the moment. I don't feel I have any other choice.

If you were to ask me at this point what I am thinking I would likely reply with something like, "I think I'll get good and drunk and go down to the Muskrats and punch somebody in the nose." After being rejected I have no ability to change how I feel, apart from what I *do* or *think* . But I have almost complete ability to change what I do and some ability to change what I think. So, knowing of my consuming interest in rhododendrons, you might tell me about a new hybrid of yours that just bloomed and that you believe should be a real prize winner, and you could suggest we go right now to see it while it is still in full, glorious bloom. I might continue to depress, but I can separate my thoughts and actions from my feelings and you might divert my mind to the new subject and get me away from thinking only about my misery and that bottle of bourbon. There are a great many things I can *do*, regardless of how I *feel*.

The important lesson here is that since we always have control over the doing component of our behavior, if we markedly change that component, we cannot avoid changing the thinking, feeling and physiological components as well. In the above example, if I continue to depress and anger over my rejection by the Muskrats there is little chance that I am going to help my cause in any way. After months of sitting and depressing, perhaps complaining to my wife and friends, drinking whiskey, I would still not be involved in the Muskrats. On the other hand, I might join the Rhododendron Society or any number of other organizations, where I would find new friends, learn new things, develop new interests. The more actively we pursue a new activity the more likely will the anger and depression dissipate, until finally they will become only a dim, although perhaps unpleasant memory. Think back to the last time you depressed and remember how little your complaining about your predicament helped your situation but how new activities enabled you to get over it.

Since we choose our behaviors, and they don't just happen to us, in the illustration involving my rejection by the Muskrats I could have chosen a number of other behaviors instead of depressing. There is anger, tension, fear, despondency, irritation, resentment, migraine and a host of other miserable states. But depression is by far the most often chosen. Now why would any reasonably intelligent person deliberately choose such a miserable behavior? It at first glance doesn't seem to make any sense at all, but when you look closer it appears more logical.

First of all, it helps to keep anger under control and anger is often terribly destructive. Suppose I had chosen anger and had followed my first impulse to go down to the Muskrats and punch somebody in the nose. No doubt I'd have been battered in return and likely would have ended up in jail or gotten sued for thousands of dollars or both, none of which would have furthered my cause. Anger is a quick, active behavior that usually makes a situation worse, while depressing moves more slowly, giving us more time to figure things out and perhaps find a solution that might work.

Secondly, depression is probably the most effective device we have for getting attention and help. We could just ask someone for help, but most of us are afraid of being refused. Besides, it would be an admission of weakness, thus frustrating our need for power. Depressing is a way of asking for help and at the same time preserving our self-esteem by denying we need it.

Thirdly, depressing helps to excuse us for being unwilling to do something more effective; it can be an excuse for fear or ineffectiveness or both. While we may feel we ought to be doing something more constructive, feeling the way we do it is hard to get started. We would prefer that others help us out and solve our problem.

Finally, depressing helps us to gain powerful control. I had an aunt who lived in a charming bungalow overlooking the Pacific Ocean, with a view you wouldn't believe. She was retired on Social Security and had a loving husband who also had a retirement income so money was no problem. In fact, upon her death money was found stashed in the deep freeze, under her mattress and in various locations throughout the house and garage.

One soon learned upon visiting her to **never, never** ask how thing were going or how she was feeling. But even without this lead, she always managed to guide the conversation to her pain, her many illnesses, her unhappiness, her unrelenting misery. Her poor husband had never read Control Theory so didn't realize that she was simply controlling him and half the neighbors, and anyone else who would listen to her woes, by choosing to depress. She smoked constantly, took twenty-seven pills every day, seldom got out of her reclining chair except to go to the bathroom or to bed, had her meals served to her in her chair, yet no doctor had found any physical basis for her complaints. Finally her muscles atrophied from lack of use and she was moved to a rest home where she soon passed away, probably in total despair. I have frequently thought of the terrible waste that was her life. But while she lived she had total control over her husband, who good-naturedly tolerated her behavior, thinking it to be inescapable.

Alarming statistics are now being generated on the incidence of alcoholism among older adults, people without a previous history of substance abuse. It is believed that a leading factor is depression. While depression may be temporarily relieved by alcohol, unfortunately it returns with a vengeance the next day. Miserable as depression may be, it often seems like the best answer one can come up with at the time and it often serves its purpose until a better choice is selected. Too often if a better choice is not made, the ultimate choice is suicide.

So far we have learned that we choose all our behaviors and that for various reasons we often choose those that seem effective at the time and are the best we can come up with at the time but that are less effective than others we could choose. Our behaviors are composed of two general types, organized behaviors and behaviors that are in a constant state of reorganization. Organized behaviors are those we use day after day to maintain control of our lives and from which we always try to select the best possible behavior to satisfy a current picture in our album. The other type of behaviors is our source of creativity and contains the building blocks of all behaviors, a kind of churning pot of disorganized behavioral material, of potential actions that are in a constant state of reorganiztion. From this ongoing stream of reorganization come new behaviors that are available for us to try if we pay attention to them and decide which of them may help us to gain or regain control over our lives.

Because we are constantly reorganizing, our chances of finding creative behaviors that will help us achieve control is greatly increased. When a behavior helps us to achieve increased control it is stored in the behavioral system as an organized behavior, ready to use wherever it may work. The unrelenting frustrations of daily living cause us to make constant demands upon our behavioral system for new behaviors to help us remain well organized and effective.

To illustrate, Steve, an attorney acquaintance, became disenchanated with the practice of law and its constant wear and tear on his nervous system, its demands on his time day and night, its deprivation of his family of his companionship, the uncertainties of his income and the constant spiraling costs of library, secretary, office rent and other expenses. He was only fifty years of age and knew that his income was only now beginning to climb and he could look forward to financial success in a short time, but that this would inevitably increase the demands on his time and increase the stress level. He had been raised on a small farm and somewhere in the back of his mind had for years had momentary thoughts of how wonderfully relaxing that life had been. But he had chosen law, had invested a lot of time and money in achieving his status as a lawyer, had developed a life style and friends accordingly, all things he could never give up. Steve's **organized** behaviors were to go to the office every work day, talk to clients, develop cases, present cases to the court, argue to the jury, get drunk on Saturday nights to ease the stress and sleep Sunday mornings while his wife and children went to church.

One Sunday morning while having a solitary cup of coffee and nursing a hangover it suddenly occurred to Steve that his expensive home was almost paid for and he had a substantial equity in it, probably enough to purchase a small acreage out of town. He had enough building experience that he felt confident he could build a house with a little help and advice from his building contractor brother. Country was certainly a preferable place to raise children. He had always dreamed of being self-sufficient, of raising his own animals for food, of having a vegetable garden and orchard. **Why not!**

When Mary and the kids returned from church expecting to find Steve stretched out on the davenport nursing a headache they were instead met by a radiant middle-aged man they hardly recognized. Steve's creative system had functioned; he had **reorganized.** His enthusiasm was contagious, and the more he explained his plan to the family the more excited they became. Mary rejoiced at the prospect of having her husband nearby more of the time, enjoying family picnics, working together to plant a garden, raising livestock. She would have no more worries about his stress level, the drinking and the danger of a heart attack. The kids envisioned a pony and perhaps ducks and other animals. Steve knew his need for alcohol was now no longer controlling and that his health would prosper from working outside and living in a healthier environment. Of course it would be uphill financially, but working together he and Mary could, and would, pull it off.

Creativity is only valuable if we can convince others that it is correct. People do not easily give up their old, well established behaviors for new ones. Steve was fortunate in having a family that readily agreed with his decision. He developed an interest in decorative plants and he and his family eventually established on their small suburban acreage a very successful mail order nursery, shipping plants all over the world. Steve remains sober to this day.

It is important to distinguish this case from a similar set of circumstances involving a sudden decision to move to a new or different location or occupation. In traditional alcohol parlance such a move is often referred to as a "geographic cure," an effort to escape one's troublesome environment on the assumption that in the new situation alcohol will no longer be a problem. Such moves are seldom planned adequately and are acts of desperation, with little consideration for long term effects on the drinker or his family, and with little thought to consequences. Such a move is certainly creative but lacks the element of responsibility that is required for it to succeed. In the case of Steve and Mary, while the decision was made by Steve rather suddenly, it was in line with his background in farm living, had been in his mind for a considerable period of time, was within his financial capabilities and offered a better life for his family as well as for himself personally.

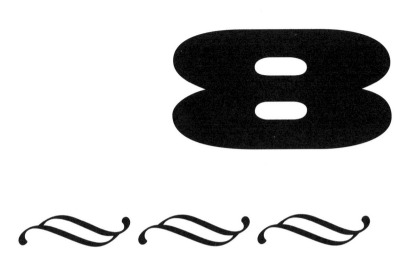

CHEMICAL CONTROL

As mentioned earlier in this book, alcohol is not necessarily a bad substance. Most users drink in moderation as an aid to conversation, a relaxant, an appetite enhancer, a social stimulant. Recent medical research seems to indicate that one or two drinks each day may help to prevent heart attacks and strokes. The old idea that mild drinking inevitably escalates into problem drinking and eventual alcoholism has now been thoroughly discredited. Beyond moderate use, however, lie serious problems.

Any sudden increase in love, power, fun or freedom is accompanied by a burst of pure pleasure. Good feelings are always a part of any effective, need-fulfilling behavior. We assume we are in control of our lives when we feel good, and we are with one important exception: when we choose to ingest addictive drugs. As Dr. Glasser states, "When drugs like heroin, alcohol, cocaine. . . reach our brain, we may, for a short time, feel ecstatic. The quick, intense pleasure that we experience feels very much like the pure, intense pleasure we feel when we suddenly take control of our lives. When we feel this drug-induced burst of pleasure, we almost always fail to realize that even though we may feel ecstatic, our lives are always seriously out of control."

Alcohol, more than any other drug, when not used in moderation, gives the user a quick and powerful sense of control. It is unique in that it is the only drug that acts to increase a sense of control that is actually being lost. Also, alcohol often leads its users to do something active rather than to remain passive as is usual with other drugs. These factors may account for the fact that a large percentage of automobile accidents involve at least one driver who has overindulged in alcohol. We frequently see patrons of taverns "peel out" at a high rate of speed when leaving the parking lot. Domestic violence such as wife beating and child sexual abuse is very often a product of alcoholic overindulgence.

A substantial percentage of criminal activity is presaged by a drinking bout. Alcohol creates feelings of invincibility. One of the author's law clients was convicted of stealing a large safe. He and a partner spent the evening drinking but ran out of funds. They went to a hardware store next door to the tavern, broke the lock on a back door, rolled a 1,000 pound safe from the front window back through the store to a loading platform in the rear, all under a glaring flood light. They rolled the safe into the back of their pick-up truck and drove up a narrow logging road near town, where they proceeded, in plain view of the road, to peel the safe. They were of course seen by a number of passers-by and reported to the police, who easily caught them in the act. Under the influence of alcohol they hadn't considered they would undoubtedly be observed at some point.

Alcohol is not a natural pleasure drug like cocaine and heroin, which imitate the opiate like chemicals secreted by the brain. Rather, it provides a sense of control that the user cannot distinguish from effective need satisfaction. The pleasure experienced, therefore, is from the user's own endorphins that are always secreted when we sense we are in control. In one sense this is most fortunate since the alcoholic, when he stops drinking and is able to satisfy his needs without alcohol, has no difficulty feeling good. Users of heroin and cocaine, on the other hand, have learned to depend on the artificial opiates to make them feel good and gradually lose the ability to feel good without the drug.

Alcohol is considered by some to be the most dangerous of all the common drugs, partly because of the way it acts on us but mostly because its heavy use is so socially acceptable. Its effects are insidious. If one drink feels good, the drinker reasons that four would make him feel four times as good. The more he drinks the greater the sense of control he experiences, yet in fact the less control he actually has. The author would never have learned to dance had he not had the assistance of alcohol, yet his typical dancing experience found him passed out in the back seat of some automobile long before the dance ended. Unfortunately this experience didn't deter him from the same behavior at the next dance.

Alcohol gives the user the feeling that all his needs are fulfilled— the powerless become powerful, the lonely become sociable, the wallflower becomes fun loving and gregarious, the meek become pugnacious, the tongue-tied become voluble, the nerd becomes a romantic hero, the awkward become Arthur Murray ballroom dancers. Only when the drug wears off does the user realize that he has been out of control. Since he wants to regain the control he has lost he drinks again as soon as possible, only to repeat the cycle over and over. Eventually he may realize that he has not been in control at all, but often by then he has become addicted.

Commonly persons with a serious drinking problem have "the hair of the dog" the morning following a binge, this being a term for having more alcohol to "knock the edge off" the hangover. It is usually effective in temporarily easing the hangover but simply prolongs the problem since the alcohol consumed the night before has not had a chance to be metabolized by the body.

How does one master the technique of maintaining moderation in his drinking? The problem many drinkers face is to maintain the delicate balance between just enough and too much. Just enough may well cause the drinker to be more fun, a better conversationalist, a more relaxed companion. But as he gains confidence he may tend to lose the ability to stop at the point where this mild condition is helpful and attractive. When faced with a family or business crisis he may be particularly vulnerable to overindulgence, since alcohol gives him the feeling that he is really in control of a difficult situation. In the following chapters we will discuss means of avoiding most crises and of substituting more responsible behaviors in crises and high stress situations.

ALTERNATIVES

Since we have learned that we do not do as others want us to do unless it coincides with the picture in our head, that is to say with what we want to do, if you are a person with a drinking problem, you now know there is no way in this world that anyone else can stop or limit your drinking behavior other than to lock you up in an alcohol free environment. Even then you would have to be closely supervised, for you, an experienced drinker and ingenious to the end, would find some way to ferment your daily bread and water rations along with your shoelaces, into some kind of drinkable brew. Wardens have for many years been awed by the ability of some inmates of prisons to rig up inventive contraptions for brewing cereal or fruit left over from meals into a potent beverage called "pruno."

But the human will is such that if you were to direct it toward the goal of controlling or eliminating your consumption of alcohol, its strength is equally awesome. If you have decided for certain that you **want** to give up alcohol, and I mean **really** want to give up alcohol, then there is nothing that will or can force you to take a drink, for **you will do what you want**

to do. There are many fortunate people who, having lived many years in an alcoholic fog, are able to commit themselves to a life of sobriety and succeed admirably. I have known quite a few and I respect them greatly. It truly can be done. My father, my uncle, my brother and both my wife's parents are among those who accomplished this worthwhile goal, and all did it without the aid of any outside agency or treatment facility.

Mike, an acquaintance who has now passed away, one evening told me his story of alcoholism and spontaneous recovery. He was raised back East and at about sixteen years of age hit the road to work the harvest fields in the midwest. In those days such people were called "bums." They had no permanent addresses, lived from hand to mouth, drank heavily whenever the means was at hand. They traveled on railroad box cars, running the risk of severe injury and arrest by the railroad "dicks," but many of them saw no other option. They loved freedom, fun, occasional power if serving as foreman or supervisor and through hard work kept their bodies in reasonably good shape. They worked when work was available, often drank when it was not.

Harvest workers would go to town on pay day and blow their wages on bread, baloney and beer, load it all in a boxcar and head for the next town. It didn't really matter where the train stopped; any town would do. Then the cycle repeated over and over throughout the harvest season.

Mike eventually drank his way through California, Oregon, Washington, and Idaho, worked in cement work, logging, mining and various odd jobs, until eventually he ended up in Alaska where he became involved in a fraudulent housing scheme and spent three years in the federal prison on McNeil Island as a result. Paroled from McNeil Island he got a job as deck hand on a tug boat on the Columbia River out of

Portland, Oregon. After a short time he worked for a carnival, guessing people's weight (which he said is a real con), then was again arrested, this time for writing bad checks. He was offered a choice of going to a mental hospital in Wyoming for treatment of his alcoholism and he accepted.

Mike claimed the treatment program was non-existent. It was merely a pretext for putting the inmates to work on the hospital grounds without any pay. But he loved the work, he did a good job and the staff showed their appreciation. Mike felt this was the turning point in his life. He was just plain tired of drinking and decided to quit. That was in 1962, and he never took another drink after that time.

Mike lost one leg which he believed was a result of frostbite while riding a train in freezing weather, and another while in the hospital in Wyoming as a result of diabetes, but as long as I knew him he didn't consider himself particularly handicapped. He scooted around on a board with rollers under it as he tended his garden, and with his artificial legs he could drive his specially equipped car and even walk up and down stairs. He served as a senior volunteer for many years before his death. He often said his only regret was the years he had wasted on alcohol.

Mike attributed his ability to give up alcohol to the fact that he had reached a position in his life where he was with people who respected him, who acknowledged his accomplishments, who encouraged him to take control of his life and who genuinely believed in him. It appeared to me he had found a way to meet his basic needs without alcohol. While Mike was able to make this transition without the need for counseling or therapy as such, many of the drinkers I've known and counseled have wanted or needed help, and I respect them equally. There's nothing wrong with seeking and accepting all the help you can get. However, you must keep in mind that no helper, no minister, no counselor, no AA sponsor, no psychiatrist, no friend, not even a "Higher Power" is going to control your drinking; only you have that power. The bottom line is that you, the drinker, must make a decision and commit yourself to a goal, then achieve it. The helpers can only stand by and support you in your effort, offering a word of advice and encouragement now and then and perhaps teaching you behaviors that would better fulfill your needs than alcohol.

In Chapters Four and Five we have considered the various techniques and concepts that have been developed and are available to assist the alcohol abuser in his attempt to control or terminate his drinking behaviors. How does one decide which technique to use? While AA is free, some of the others are quite expensive and time consuming — and there is no assurance that any of them will work for you. Perhaps by carefully reading the foregoing descriptions you may find some that have no appeal whatsoever, while one or two may look interesting. Or maybe you will decide that you are ready to take control of your life and can go it alone. Many do. Those who succeed are the ones who truly want to make a change and who willingly commit themselves to it. I believe that the principles of Reality Therapy and Control Theory can be of great help to these people. The purpose of this book is to make these concepts available to you.

DO NOT GIVE UP! If you do try it alone and feel at any time that it isn't working, please do not hesitate to seek help. It's never too late to ask for help, and there is no shortage of people willing to give it. It is not easy to change any behavior of long standing, and it is particularly difficult to break an addiction, as you may suffer extreme physical discomfort as well as emotional distress. It is important that you consult a medical doctor if you encounter physical or severe emotional problems. There are professional Reality Therapists in the field if that appeals to you, and while they are not plentiful since this concept is fairly new, they are available, although you may have to search them out.

If you are the spouse or significant other of an alcoholic or problem drinker and are at your wit's end, do not try to handle the situation yourself by argument, persuasion, badgering, anger, withholding love, etc. All these tactics are losers. Get help from a professional counselor and/or attend a meeting of Al-Anon, a support group for people closely related to alcoholics. At Al-Anon you will meet other people in your situation and you will learn how and where to get help in intervening in your alcoholic's drinking behaviors, as well as ceasing your own behaviors in "enabling" the alcoholic to pursue his drinking career. These are both very valuable techniques in helping to get an alcoholic in a state of mind where he may decide to change his drinking behaviors, but the process often needs professional guidance. You will find Al-Anon listed in the Yellow Pages of your telephone directory under "Alcoholism." It does not help to nag or to constantly remind the alcoholic of his shortcomings; he's already painfully aware of them. It merely increases his "error" and provides another reason to use his favorite pain killer, alcohol.

Many marriages that begin with optimism eventually fail, with excessive drinking on the part of one or both spouses. Alcohol is usually blamed for the failure of the marriage, yet perhaps the drinking is merely symptomatic of serious underlying problems in the marriage itself, problems which, if seriously and thoughtfully resolved, might cause the marriage relationship to recover its initial health, whereupon the drinking might well diminish or even terminate. Dr. Glasser has just published a book that can be of great assistance in assessing the extent of marriage problems and in guiding the participants in seeking solutions. It is highly recommended to families experiencing alcohol related problems. The book is *STAYING TOGETHER: A Control Theory Guide to a Lasting Marriage* (N.Y.: Harper Collins, 1995.)

The vast majority of alcohol consumers in this country drink socially and with no significant problems. A study a few years ago indicated that a drink or two each day was probably beneficial and a very recent study established the fact that a half bottle of wine per day cuts the risk of heart disease in half and probably has other helpful health benefits as well. But wine consumption needs to be spread out and usually taken with meals. Three bottles of wine consumed on Saturday night, for example, would have a negative effect. It appears questionable as of this writing whether beer and hard liquor, even in moderate quantities, provide similar benefits.

If you are a social drinker and want to find out how much you drink, or if you are a mild problem drinker and would like to try to become and remain a social drinker, then you should, and perhaps can, learn the techniques of controlled drinking. If you are alcoholic or have a serious drinking problem, then it has not traditionally been recommended that you attempt controlled drinking. New studies have seemed to indicate, however, that many heavy drinkers who attempted total abstinence failed in that goal but succeeded in establish-ing moderate   drinking habits.[35] These studies were tightly controlled and comparatively short in duration, so it remains to be seen what the long term outcome will be. It seems reasonable to assume that if the abuser not only gave up heavy drinking but found other more responsible means of satisfying his needs, then he should be able to enjoy a few recreational drinks. But the concept certainly runs counter to the preachments of Alco-holics Anonymous and the belief of many experienced thera-pists who have found that an alcoholic's return to drinking in any amount reinstates the addictive behavior in full vigor.

CONTROLLED DRINKING

Various strategies have been developed for controlling alcohol consumption, all consisting of basically the same components, namely the setting of goals or limits, the monitoring of consumption, periodic assessment of trends and results and either rewards for success or possible restructuring of goals. The table on page 13 may be consulted to determine the maximum blood alcohol content (BAC) you wish to achieve. The expected effects of various BAC levels follow the chart in narrative form. Keep in mind that the figures in the chart are approximate and that some people are particularly sensitive to alcohol's effects and may react more severely than the narrative may indicate. Only experience will tell you for sure.

Some people set a basic goal for ordinary days and a slightly higher one for special occasions like weddings. Goals should set the maximum number of drinks per day and per week and should not exceed twenty-one drinks per week, as it is

often believed that more than three drinks per day over a period
of time can be detrimental to health.

For purposes of monitoring consumption it is suggested
that you make a series of three-by-five-inch cards approximately as follows:

Date_____Occasion_____

Type (beer,wine 13%, wine 20%, 80 proof,100 proof)

1.Type_____Time_____With_____At_____
2.Type_____Time_____With_____At_____
3.Type_____Time_____With_____At_____
4.Type_____Time_____With_____At_____

Try to record all drinks when received. If that isn't possible,
estimate, but do record them. Be as specific as possible. If you
aren't sure of alcohol content, ask.

A page of cards is located at the end of this book. It may
be removed and photocopied. Carry one or more cards with
you at all times. Note the two admonitions on the bottom of the
card: Record all drinks when received and if you do not know
the alcohol content of each drink, ask someone. Do find out and
record it eventually. It is also quite important to record who you
are drinking with and where you drink. It may appear over a
period of time that you tend to drink more or violate your limits
when with a particular person or at a particular place. Keep the
cards and review them periodically, preferably weekly, to note
trends. Once you have self-monitored for a while it will become
a habit. Intentional failure to record drinks or other information
defeats the purpose of this exercize, and makes it of no value to
you or anyone else.

You needn't be embarrassed by self-monitoring. Your real friends will understand and be supportive while your old drinking buddies may feel threatened by it at first. You may occasionally meet up with a person who insists you drink with him even though it may violate your limits or your spacing of drinks. You must be assertive and stand your ground. If you give in under any circumstances you have abdicated your control. Remember that only you can decide whether or not to take a drink — you are not at the mercy of outside forces, even if they weigh 300 pounds and play wide receiver for the Rams.

Many teachers of controlled drinking recommend that a successful period of monitoring and controlling be followed by a reward, such as an activity, experience or object that the controller does not usually get, but obviously not in the form of additional drinks. The reward must be something reasonably obtainable by the person.

If controlled drinking doesn't work out for you do not consider the experience a failure. It may well be successful in the sense that it may indicate beyond any doubt that you have a more severe drinking problem than you realized and that total abstinence is a more realistic goal.

Many therapists are trained in the techniques of controlled drinking and can offer advice and support. Meanwhile, here are some success oriented suggestions. Some may seem a bit redundant, but I believe they are worth repeating:

1. DO make a firm commitment to accurately and faithfully monitor your drinking before you undertake this enterprise. Remember it is intended to eventually help you fulfill one or more of your needs.

2. DO carry a supply of cards with you at all times and make entries **before** you consume each drink if possible. Accuracy often diminishes as BAC rises.

3. DO NOT simply forego monitoring if you forget

or inadvertently run out of cards.   Write the information on a napkin or scrap of paper and transfer it to a card later. If that is not possible, try your best to remember the information until you have sober access to cards and then make the entries.

4. DO space your drinks to maintain your desired BAC at or below your goal.

5. DO sip your drinks rather than gulping them. It spreads the consumption out over a greater time period, thus diminishing the urge to order more drinks.

6. DO try to switch from concentrated drinks such as martinis or "shots" to mixed drinks, beer or table wine. The more dilute drinks contain about the same amount of alcohol as the concentrated ones but enable you to spread consumption over a greater time period.

7. DO allow a period of time to pass after finishing one drink before ordering another.

8. DO avoid drinking at places where you tend to over consume, or if you must go there, sit in a different place, play shuffleboard, make changes from your usual patterns.

9. DO avoid drinking with old drinking buddies who tend to overindulge. They may mean well and may be dear to you but they can subtly undermine your best intentions.

10. DO avoid drinking soon after a crisis situation, such as a family argument, loss of a job or rejection by a lover. At these times your resolve may weaken dramatically.

11. DO develop new interests and activities such as hobbies, jogging, hiking, tennis and other things that do not ordinarily involve drinking, and try getting acquainted with new people who drink moderately or not at all. It's amazing how interesting and supportive they can be.

12. DO seek help from a qualified counselor or therapist if you have difficulty with any aspect of this program. It is a sign of moral strength, not weakness, to accept assistance rather than

to give up.

13. DO NOT give in to badgering, argument, ridicule or other efforts of others to cause you to violate your limits. You are a free person, firmly in control and subject to outside influences but **not** outside control. **Only you make your decisions.**

14. DO hold to your decision to control your drinking. The purpose of this decision and its implementation is to learn to substitute more appropriate behaviors for inappropriate ones, and only by this means do you learn, in all facets of your life, to better fulfill your basic needs. **However,**

15. DO NOT become discouraged and give up entirely if it appears that, despite your most sincere efforts, you are convinced this technique does not work for you. One of the most promising results of a controlled drinking approach is that it frequently indicates a person may have a more severe drinking problem than previously realized and that a more realistic approach is total abstinence. DO NOT automatically reject that possibility. It will now be explored.

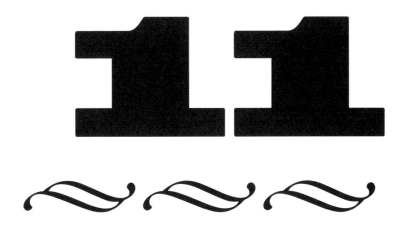

ABSTINENCE

It is very difficult, if not impossible, to just "quit" — anything. It leaves a void in your life where that activity has been, and if the activity has been a frequent one such as smoking or drinking, you find yourself constantly reaching for the pocket where the cigarettes are usually kept or yearning for some fluid pouring down your throat. For weeks after the author stopped smoking he kept reaching for his shirt pocket, particularly after meals.

It is considerably easier to substitute a new behavior for the one you are giving up, like perhaps drinking a caffeinated beverage after a meal instead of smoking a cigarette. It's a mild stimulant but will help you break the habit of the cigarette ritual — removing the pack from your pocket, removing the cigarette from the pack, tapping it, lighting it, puffing it, depositing the ash in an ash tray. But the application of this principle to abstinence from alcohol becomes very complex. To an alcoholic, giving up alcohol is not the giving up of a single behavior but of a mixture of behaviors, a whole way of life, in fact. So it is not surprising that so many people refuse to give up alcohol. They simply don't choose to make that many changes. But change they must if they are to successfully deal with their problems so as to begin to satisfy their needs. Every problem drinker, if he will really search his heart and conscience, will find that he has been unable to satisfy one or more of his basic needs in a satisfactory way and that drinking was the activity he chose in his desperate efforts to deal with the pain.

Lets explore that a bit. You'll never know what other people really think of you as a person since that is in their "personal world" and you are not a party to it. But they have many ways of letting you peek into their world and it matters tremendously what you perceive others think of you and how you think of yourself.

When I attended high school in a small town in the Midwest I was class president every year, consistently had the highest grades in my class, lettered in every athletic activity in the school, was considered good looking and personable and didn't have any trouble getting dates. Eventually I found a girl friend that I loved and who said she loved me. Obviously I appeared to be worthwhile to others and had the ability to love and be loved. But I began to drink very early. So what was missing? Probably partly that I didn't feel worthwhile to **myself**. I was six feet, six inches tall in a world inhabited by people under six feet and was frequently reminded of the difference by comments like, "How's the weather up there?" or "Hand me down a match." We were very poor and I usually wore bib overalls to functions where other kids wore slacks and shirts because that's all I had.

So I had the **perception** that I was probably not very worthwhile to others, and you will remember that all I know of the outside world is what I perceive of it, not what it truly is, necessarily. And I **perceived** that I was too tall and wore the wrong clothes, among other things. In my effort to reduce this "error" I drank, for when I was intoxicated it didn't seem to matter that I was too tall, that my clothes were different, that I was awkward on the dance floor or, for that matter, that my speech was slurred, that I staggered or lost my balance, or that I said things that were inappropriate or offensive to others. I would only regret that the next day, perhaps, because my male peers would comment, "Boy, were you ever loaded,"with an approving grin.

But I learned from these experiences. I learned that if I became uncomfortable in a social situation it was okay to block out the pain with alcohol and experience pleasure as well, just as I learned soon after my birth that crying got warmth and food. And that knowledge served faithfully in my "memory bank" for many years, took me through the army and World War II and social experiences in many strange lands and through many traumatic events. It took me through college and casual dating, through law school and its attending social functions, through the beginnings of a law practice and its social functions and the trauma of the court room (although I never entered a courtroom under the influence, I often drank heavily for days before in apprehension, and for days after, either in celebration or agony, depending on the outcome). It was my true friend, always there, always reliable to mask the pain and provide a degree of pleasure.

You will note, of course, the word "mask," for that is what alcohol does. It does not kill the pain nor dispose of it — it simply allows you to ignore the pain for the moment. It fools you into thinking that you are in good control of your life. But unfortunately my basic need to feel worthwhile to myself and to others was no closer to fulfillment when I walked out of that bar on the morning of Feb. 1, 1959, than it was when I took my first drink at the age of twelve years. In fact it was much farther from fulfillment, knowing that my often irresponsible behavior had harmed other people and caused my parents, children and wife heartache, embarrassment and dread.

My decision to give up alcohol was not a simple decision to quit drinking. It was preceded by two significant events. A week or so earlier I was driving my pickup down the freeway with a friend at my side and a bottle under the seat. We were going deer hunting in the mountains some distance from home. It was very early in the morning and we were both very quiet. I suddenly realized that I had absolutely no recollection of the last ten or twelve miles and it scared the hell out of me! It was my first experience with "blacking out." Up until that time I had always remembered everything I had ever done, even when intoxicated.

The next day I went to a doctor, told him of the experience and had a brief examination. He informed me that I was a good candidate for a fatal heart attack if I continued to live the way I had been. The episode with the vodka martini a couple of days later was merely the straw that broke the camel's back. Faced with this new information I decided what I wanted to do and I made a commitment: **that I would never again consume alcohol in any form.**

WHAT DO YOU WANT?

The answer to that question is crucial to anyone's attempt to control alcohol or to remove it from his or her life because no person is going to make any major change in his life unless that is what he wants to do. In control theory terms we have to find a new picture for our personal picture album that better fulfills our needs than the picture of alcohol. We just do not do what others want us to do or order us to do unless it coincides, as it sometimes does, with what we want to do.

There is a law that says we must stop at all red lights. We might resent it or feel it's unnecessary, but the alternative is jail or a fine so we decide we'd rather stop at the red light than go to jail or pay a fine. So we decide we want to stop, and we do — usually. But if our wife is with us on the way to the hospital and about to deliver a baby we may decide we'd rather pay the fine or go to jail than try to deliver the baby ourself in the car, so we decide we want to run the red light, and we do. We decide what we want and we act on it.

If you want to continue problem drinking behavior that is your right and your choice. It's still legal in this country and if it's what you want to do you will undoubtedly find a way to do it. There really isn't much anyone else can do to cause you to make a decision to give it up. As has already been pointed out you have the power to give up alcohol but only if that's what **you** want to do. But I can't make you want to do it.

Much current research is directed at trying to find ways to motivate the problem drinker to quit drinking and most of the treatment methods are preoccupied with attempts at motivation. But it's a hard thing to teach or force or mandate. It has to come from within so it's a very individual, personal thing. I was motivated by a blackout, a doctor's diagnosis and an overfull martini glass. Many alcoholics have survived much more than that without its diminishing their appetite for booze. When you decide to commit to a life of sobriety, more than likely you will have been motivated by some sort of life crisis. Historically, most "spontaneous remissions," in the books and in my personal experience, followed a crisis of unusually serious proportions. But a significant number just tapered off their drinking and finally stopped because it no longer fulfilled any need.

Most problem drinkers I have known who seemed to want to quit also seemed not to want to quit. This condition is called ambivalence, and it's not unusual when we think of making a drastic change in our life. It's not always easy to detect this ambivalence unless you know what you're looking for. Often it's disguised in a phrase like "one day at a time." The theory is that the person can only commit himself to sobriety **today** and that he must renew that vow each day as long as he wants to stay sober. That, of course, leaves tomorrow, or some tomorrow, open for drinking, which usually occurs. I have rarely found a person who had been subjected to this philosophy who could even conceive of committing him or herself to a **life** of sobriety, although supposedly that was what was being sought at the time. "One day at a time" has entered their memory bank and has served most of them well, through many AA meetings and often through various treatment facilities and a continuing life of alcohol abuse. You may remember from Eric's story earlier in this book, how he stated he was willing to commit himself to a life of sobriety but only for a day at a time. A perfect example of ambivalence.

Another good dodge is the ambiguity of the word "quit." Several of my friends have announced their intention to quit drinking, and when I found them drinking at a later date they seemed amazed that I could have thought they meant forever. They had quit but then had started again. I guess that made sense to them because it was what they wanted to do but I found it confusing. What these ambivalent people appear to really want is not to terminate their drinking behavior but merely to interrupt it for a while. And even that has some value. It may get their physical health back into a semblance of order before they go back to drinking.

To me, having to get up **each morning** and make a pledge not to drink that day would be unacceptable. Even if it worked it would mean thinking seriously of alcohol at least once each day for the rest of my life. If I wanted to refrain from alcohol all the rest of my life it would seem appropriate to do it all at once, put the thing behind me and eventually forget about it and go on to better things. People who claim they want to live a life of sobriety yet refuse to give up alcohol for the rest of their lives are, I believe, not facing reality and are behaving irresponsibly. They cannot drink and not drink at the same time; it's impossible. They have been failing to fulfill their basic needs, yet are refusing to even try to learn new and better behaviors. Is this judgmental and moralistic? You bet it is, for morals, standards, values and right or wrong behaviors are all intimately related to our ability to satisfy our needs and take effective control of our lives.

Well now, if you have decided that you have not been able to satisfactorily fulfill your needs, but that that is what you want to do, what efforts have you made so far? Have you tried controlled drinking? Have you tried quitting for one day at a time? Have you tried turning the whole thing over to a "Higher Power," and asking Him to solve it for you? Have you tried chemical aversion therapy, or electric shock aversion therapy, or perhaps psychoanalysis? Have you been thrown into jail to "teach you a lesson"? Have you tried just plain quitting, cold turkey? Perhaps several of the above? Did any of it work? If so, congratulations. But if not, and I suspect you wouldn't be reading this otherwise, let's take a look at some things you might consider doing differently that can help you toward your goal so that you no longer need alcohol to mask your pain and frustration.

First, it is essential that you have at least one person in your life (and preferably more) for whom you care and who genuinely cares for you. Parents are usually good candidates for this position as they usually love their children in spite of the mistakes they may have made. If they have rejected you, try them again. They are usually quite forgiving when they realize you are now doing the right thing. Many of my alcoholic clients had totally lost contact with their families and had been "on the road" for months or years and had formed no new and meaningful relationships, so many hours were spent in reestablishing communication with parents or other relatives. Often these were the only likely persons with whom the client might establish a genuinely close relationship, and it always proved worth the time and effort.

If you are affiliated with a church your pastor may have some suggestions. But always keep in mind that whoever you select must themselves be in touch with reality and able to fulfill their own needs reasonably well. This would probably rule out old drinking friends no matter how well you relate to them, unless they have already successfully dealt with their own drinking problems. Be sure you have this step well in hand before undertaking the next.

Second, it is essential that you declare to yourself, to every acquaintance and to the world in general **that you are through with alcohol.** This is a solemn commitment and unless you **want** to make it, it probably will not work. You will only do what you want to do. If you find this step unacceptable then you are probably not ready for a **life** of sobriety and might consider going back to "one day at a time." You cannot take charge of your life until you decide what you want to do. You cannot succeed in eliminating alcohol from your life so long as you maintain ambivalent feelings about it. On the other hand, if you **can** take this step you will find it extremely rewarding in the long run but only the first step in a series of changes, none of which is easy but all of which help you **take control of your life**. Once you have taken this step you can forever forget having to "quit drinking"; you have done it, once and for all.

It may well be very difficult for you to take this second step. You will not be alone as you will note from the following quote from another author's work on alcohol abuse: "It is not the thought of quitting drink that bothers alcoholics, since they have imagined that thousands of times, but the notion of never drinking again. That is almost incomprehensible. Surely, at some future time they can risk it — so they tell themselves — when their lives have been set in order, when their thoughts have been straightened out, when they are wise enough to avoid the mistakes of their past drinking bouts, when they no longer crave alcohol, when medical science comes up with a new cure, and so on. . . .they want to believe they have learned from their mistakes. It is this unstated, usually unrecognized expectation about their drinking that often keeps the embers of desire alive and maintains their vulner- ability. If alcoholics truly believe that under no circum- stances, at no time, at no place, and with no exceptions do they have the option of returning to drink, then the voice of seduction will be completely stilled." [36]

When you have taken this second step you will feel good about yourself, as well you should. It is a real accom- plishment, and one you may be proud of. But do not be over confident; there is still a long way to go. You will feel cravings for a time and almost overwhelming desires to have perhaps just one drink, but you must not and need not. It could destroy the progress you have made and your newly gained feelings of real control. It is amazing how much power you will gain as you are able to say to yourself (and others), "I've had no alcohol for one month," then one year, then ten years, then thirty. Remember, you are in control and you are not subject to outside controls unless you choose to be. You can and will do what you choose to do and you have chosen to give up alcohol for the rest of your life and have made a firm commit- ment to that choice. Some people at this point may slip and take a drink. If this should happen, please consider it a learning experience and return to your sobriety rather than abandoning your goal. Strong people in this position are sometimes vulnerable for a moment, but it need not be the end of your effort. Those of us who have been through the mill will admire your guts for being human enough to relapse but powerful enough to persevere. But keep in mind that your progress will be faster and smoother if you can prevent relapses.

Let me share with you what happened to me just after I made the commitment never again to consume alcohol in any form, and the word got around. As I mentioned earlier, I began my practice in a small firm with another firm down the hall and that the members of both drank heavily. The senior member of the firm down the hall, whom we will call Jack and with whom I drank almost constantly, offered me free use of his library, waiting room and secretary if I would rent a small vacant "cubbyhole" just off his waiting room for my private office. I accepted; it made the drinking easier, more convenient. He furnished all the booze; all I had to do was to go a block to the liquor store each day and pick up two fifths and two pints of whiskey, for which he paid. In addition there were many gifts of office furniture, fishing gear, money to buy things for my family when I was short. I was like the son he'd never had. We went to conventions together, fished and hunted together, tried cases together, went dancing together, the two families picnicked together, and so on.

When I made my commitment Jack, of course, couldn't believe I was serious. He kept telling me my resolve would last a few days and I'd be back drinking with him. He'd been through this before with other men and it always had worked out that way. At first he urged me to drink with him. Then in a few days he began demanding that I drink with him and soon advised me that either I drank with him "or else." I announced my intention to move, and now the use of the library, waiting room and secretary became "shared expense" with my being liable retroactively for my share; the various gifts had been loans to be repaid. About this time an older lawyer retired from practice so his office was available. I arranged to rent it, but I had no office furniture other than a desk and chair, no waiting room furniture, no library, no secretary and no money for any of those, let alone the rent.

I went to the bank where I had done business for several years but from which I'd never borrowed money. I told the loan officer the total story, including my drinking history (of which he was already aware, not surprisingly), my vow and why I needed the money. He loaned me a substantial sum on my signature, to my surprise and to my great relief. The word of my sobriety soon spread among those in my profession and I began getting referrals from lawyers I had always thought to be contemptuous of me. Since I no longer drank I had more time to devote to my practice. It soon built to a very successful level, and I was able to pay off the bank loan on time and thereby establish a valuable line of credit. Every step along the line my feelings of power, professional belonging and self worth rose accordingly, and with that thoughts of alcohol became less frequent. In fact, for long periods of time I didn't think about it. And what about Jack? He died many years ago of acute alcoholism, at the age of 53.

Sometimes it's still hard to believe that all that happened so many years ago, especially the drinking part. Alcohol is just not a part of my world any longer, except in my effort to help other people deal with it. Of course that does not mean there were not pressures, temptations (sometimes almost overwhelming), and urges along the way. There were plenty of those, but there are ways of dealing with them and we (you and I) will find ways to avoid some of them and cope with others.

Please believe me when I say that it becomes easier as you go along and eventually becomes a whole new way of life, rewarding, satisfying and responsible.

PERSONAL POWER

Here are some things you can do or avoid that should help you in your new way of life. First, do not hesitate to admit to yourself and to others that you have a drinking problem and are taking positive steps to eliminate it. There is nothing to be ashamed of. It has been estimated that as high as 10% of our adult population has a drinking problem, to say nothing of younger people, so it is quite probable that almost every family has a relative or close friend that drinks inappropriately. The shame is in not doing anything about it. Your old drinking friends may think you've gone out of your mind at first but will undoubtedly envy you in reality. The rest will respect you greatly, and you will find support and encouragement from many unexpected sources.

DO SOMETHING! The drinking you used to do consumed a lot of your time, energy and thoughts so you're going to have time on your hands, energy to burn and thoughts that can get you into trouble. The worst thing you can do is to sit and brood over anything. In control theory terms that is called depressing, a chosen behavior that is one of the most common behaviors but one that requires some action to dispel. I cannot stress enough the importance of keeping busy, keeping your body and mind occupied with new experiences, new information, new thoughts, new people, new activities in order that you not dwell on the loss of an old and, until now, valued friend, alcohol. Remember, you choose your behaviors, including thoughts and feelings. Take up a new hobby, such as woodworking, painting, stamp collecting, or better yet, a more active hobby such as gardening, which will encourage your creativity and give you some physical activity as well.

Most of us seem to have an inborn need to create and many hobbies satisfy this need and thereby fulfill our needs for fun, for belonging if it involves an organization as it often does, and even power if we are extraordinarily creative and become in demand as a speaker or demonstrator of our specialty. Gardening has been my personal choice, and I have just created my fifth rhododendron garden, this time about an acre in size with over 600 plants. Most were grown by my own labor so represented little investment in money. Of course there are those who think I'm a little balmy, too, for it's a tremendous amount of work but, my, you should see it in bloom in May! And the "strokes" I get from my friends and the members of the Rhododendron Society! And now after a few years I am in demand as a speaker and writer on the subject.

SET GOALS. In my group sessions I often assigned each person the task of presenting at the next session something he had always wanted to do, within his means, but that had not been accomplished. It was amazing the excitement and enthusiasm this often created. Your feelings of self worth, power and belonging are greatly enhanced by your accomplishments. To a very large extent you are what you **do** so if you want to change what you are, you must begin by changing what you do. You may sit for weeks fantasizing about how

wonderful it would be to be manager of your store or department, but fantasy does little besides entertain unless you take
positive steps to make it become reality.

Consider, then, the many alternatives you have: you
may just continue to fantasize in which case nothing much will
change; you may take some self improvement courses at the
local junior college, such as assertiveness, time management,
public speaking, communication skills; or marketing courses
such as salesmanship, economics, advertising, personnel management. Offer to put in extra time on the job to learn the
requirements of the next step up. Do a little extra on your present
job. This rarely goes unnoticed. Let your employer know your
goals and what you are doing toward preparing yourself to meet
them.

Your goals must be reasonably within your capabilities;
if you are sixty-eight years old you probably couldn't expect to
become an astronaut. They must be achievable by your own
efforts rather than dependent on someone else. "Making your
marriage work" is a laudable goal but dependent on your
spouse's participation. Praising your wife more and refusing to
criticize her would be more achievable goals; you can do them
by yourself and they would go a very long way in making your
marriage work. Your goals must be measurable, in the sense
that you will know when they have been attained. For example,
it wouldn't be realistic to set as a goal the development of a
"fine" personality since you, yourself, probably wouldn't be
able to recognize whether the goal had been attained. But it
would be appropriate to set a goal of taking a course in
"personality improvement." Satisfactory completion of the
course is within your ability to judge.

Very long term goals, such as becoming manager of
your store, should be broken down into a number of short term
goals, such as the taking of a self improvement course or

learning the operation of a single department. Once you have set a realistic goal, **do not give up**. Many will not be easy, but you will **always** feel good about having completed a goal satisfactorily and your accomplishments seldom go unnoticed by others. Feeling good about yourself and being acknowledged and respected by others are very large factors in dealing with an alcohol problem.

AVOID BEING ALONE. We are all more vulnerable when we are lonely. Encourage new friendships that do not involve alcohol and do things with the new friends. You may have to give up some of your old friends if they continue to drink. They've been used to you as a drinking person and it's hard for them to think of you otherwise. They may plead and cajole and even threaten you to get you to return to your old ways, because they are uncomfortable. But as much as you may hate to face it, these are not your true friends, unless they are willing to forego alcohol while in your presence and respect your wish to remain alcohol-free. Your real friends will want what is best for you, not just themselves, and what is best for you is non-drinking behavior.

In a while you will be able to join a group having cocktails while you have a plain soda or orange juice, but it's best to avoid such situations at first. It doesn't bother me a bit to associate with a group that is drinking alcohol while I have a soda, but it does bother some of them. I no longer find cocktail parties interesting so I usually avoid them if possible. Even after all these years people occasionally inquire why I don't join them for a drink, and I have no problem explaining that I have chosen a life of sobriety. It is interesting to watch their reactions. Most act respectful, some even a little envious. No one has ever been derisive. I've often wondered if any of them consider my inability or unwillingness to drink alcohol a weakness — a character defect. I consider it a strength.

Take the kids to a movie, take the family to church, go to athletic events with non-drinking friends, join the "Y" and take swimming, tennis or other lessons. Go to an AA meeting once in a while and see how others are coping. If you are single or divorced, join a legitimate counseling group to meet others similarly situated. Check the Yellow Pages of your telephone directory under "Counselors" for listings of available services. Volunteer your expertise and/or services to some social agency to benefit crippled children, the elderly or retarded. Get involved in an environmentally oriented group of activists. There is no end of ways to meet new people who are not involved with alcohol.

GET CONTROL of your domestic situation. Your love relationships are crucial to your ability to meet your fundamental needs. Cement them. If there are problems in one or more of your relationships, get counseling, communicate your thoughts and feelings in a positive way, show your affection, ask questions, make changes in your own behavior rather than expecting the other person to do the changing, respect the right of your significant other to feel, believe and act differently than you. Do not just sit and suffer and do not continue to "play old tapes" or rehash old arguments that are best forgotten or that have proven beyond solution in the past.

There are marriage and family counselors listed in the Yellow Pages of your telephone directory. Remember, you must be able to love and to receive love and you must have in your life at least one person who cares for you and for whom you care. Your love interest (wife or significant other) may be one of the most valuable assets in your life at this point in time, so preserve it, pamper it — and utilize it.

If you have no love relationship you may choose to create one. While this is a perfectly natural pursuit, it must be approached cautiously and responsibly, especially by the newly sober person. It is not acceptable to select another person with a drug or drinking problem or a person not fully in touch with reality and reasonably able to fulfill his or her own needs. If you end up with such a person as a mate you have double trouble. Dr. Glasser's new book *STAYING TOGETHER: A Control Theory Guide to a Lasting Marriage* (N.Y.:Harper Collins, 1995) can be of great assistance in helping you judge the likelihood of success in an anticipated marriage.

You may well be very lonely and therefore vulnerable to hasty decisions in the romantic realm so select carefully, proceed slowly and be responsible. Your entire future is at stake. Marriage is easily contracted but dissolved only with pain and great expense. Termination of an unsatisfactory love relationship is equally traumatic. So seek your love object in church, on the jogging trail, on the tennis court, at the "Y," at a PTA meeting or school function, during a volunteer assignment, but not at a bar, or singles dance or at an AA meeting. You are guaranteed no successes at the former nor failures at the latter but love is at best something of a gamble and it behooves one to consider the odds. There is a tendency among lonely people to grasp at the first romantic opportunity. Have patience; there will be another along in time.

DO NOT try to stop smoking or drinking coffee while giving up alcohol or other mind altering drugs. It has been my experience that most newly sober and clean persons smoke more tobacco and drink more coffee by far than they did when drinking and using. As we know, it is very difficult to just quit anything and much easier to substitute some other behavior, and that is exactly what you are doing when you smoke more and drink more coffee. If you are addicted to other mind altering substances in addition to alcohol, you probably cannot continue to use, say, cocaine, heroin or marijuana while giving up just alcohol. You likely cannot maintain your dedication to your new alcohol free program if you are out of your head on some other drug. You will undoubtedly need professional help with multiple addiction. It is extremely important that you not take up a new mind altering substance, such as marijuana or barbiturates, as a substitute for alcohol.

MAKE CHANGES in your life style. You cannot just go on living the same old life style, but without the alcohol. If job related stress has interfered with your ability to fulfill your needs and it appears you have been using alcohol to ease the discomfort, then it may be necessary to seek counseling in an effort to adjust to the present job, or ask your employer to change the job requirements to more nearly suit your capabilities, or ask for a transfer to a less stressful job, or even quit the job and look for another. Go to a college or trade school and prepare for a different job. Your financial situation may well dictate which alternative you choose, but choose you must. You simply cannot just continue to suffer an "error." You must choose some behavior that will create for you the perception that the job you want (outside world) and the job you have (personal world) are nearly the same or you will continue to suffer pain.

If you are living in a development or "condo" where you are constantly besieged by drinking opportunities, by all means move as quickly as possible. You will experience more than enough temptation from within without having to suffer the outside pressures of such a living arrangement. However, don't fall for the idea that all you need to do to quit drinking is to move to a different neighborhood. This is called a "geographic cure" and rarely works. If your car pool is in the habit of stopping for drinks on the way home, change transportation. If you normally have drinks with your lunch or dinner, substitute soda or juice. If that is an embarrassing departure from your normal menu selections, change restaurants.

Likewise, you cannot continue going to the same places with the same people and engaging in the same old behaviors. You need to break out of your present patterns, make new friends, find new interests, break old ties, forego old habits and make new, responsible ones. You will no longer stop at the bar on the way home from work, not even if you order a soda rather than a beer or cocktail. There are too many old friends, old habits, old memories there.

You will no longer keep beer or liquor in the refrigerator or grab a beer before sitting down to watch the Saturday game or an evening movie on TV. Indulge yourself in favorite non-alcohol beverages such as soda or fruit juices and favorite foods. We'll worry about the cholesterol and calories after the alcohol has been controlled. Keep gallons of liquids available. You've been used to something wet going down your throat. Don't try to give that up now. Just be sure it's non-alcohol.

If you have been used to doing your yard work with a can of beer in your hand, substitute a can of cola or other soft drink. Do not substitute "near beer"; it contains about one-half of one percent alcohol and could undermine your efforts.

If you can benefit from spiritual advice or if you are affiliated with a church or religious organization, seek out relationships with your pastor and other members and participate in their activities. You will undoubtedly meet old friends as well as new and interesting people and will be in an alcohol-free environment. In addition, many religious organizations offer programs in alcohol counseling and provide support groups to assist the alcoholic and those with personal or marital problems.

KEEP YOUR BODY in good physical condition. Jog, walk, run, work out with weights and/or calisthenics; play tennis, golf, handball, racquetball; swim, join an aerobic class. Do get lots of exercise. And do eat a healthful diet with plenty of vegetables and fruit as well as protein to support your exercise program. And keep your mind active by keeping up on current events, by reading magazines and books and by talking to people.

Do not be frightened of sharing your feelings and innermost thoughts or concerns with family and friends. They will be pleased to know you better and will probably share some things with you that you haven't known before. Many times when we feel "down" we immediately feel better after discussing things with another person. It feels good to get it off our chest.

Most communities of any size now have junior colleges or trade schools where classes of an amazing variety are offered at a reasonable price. Frequently available, in addition to academic courses, are practical courses such as personality improvement, communication skills, establishing new relationships, coping with divorce or separation, marriage and family, assertiveness, making friends, parenting, improving couple relationships, developing self confidence, men and women and their respective roles, etc.

HAVE SOME FUN. One of the elements that every person seems to need in his or her life is "fun." But what in the world does that word mean, anyway? Is it some activity that gives us pleasure? But then we're faced with defining the word "pleasure," for to most people it's just another word for "fun." Perhaps it's any activity that we enjoy that we don't have to do. Or maybe there's no real need to define it. One of our Supreme Court justices once said, when asked to define a certain word, "Well, I can't define it but I know it when I see it." I guess I could fall back on that because I certainly know when I've been having fun.

Fun is different things to different people. I once thought the ultimate fun was to buy a fifth of good whiskey and go out dancing on Saturday night, and when I occasionally walk into a night club or tavern on a Saturday night it appears obvious that people are still having fun doing that same sort of thing because there's a great deal of loud laughter and people are dancing and seem highly animated and joyous, normal signs of fun. Nowadays I can't imagine anything more boring. So our ideas of fun change from time to time. Many men have fun watching a football game on television on Saturday afternoon and dread or resent having to do yard work, but I would prefer to pull weeds in my garden than watch a football game. I love to write — letters, articles of all kinds, this book — but my wife would rather do most anything than write a letter.

So do what you enjoy doing so long as it doesn't interfere with anyone else's enjoyment and so long as it doesn't involve alcohol. And for the time being, it is probably best if you can enjoy doing it with someone else. Even fun is less rewarding if you're lonely.

DO NOT GIVE UP OR GIVE IN. You will be subject to enormous pressures from within and from without, but have courage. It took you many years to develop your habit and it may take many more to overcome it entirely. You can prevail but only if you resist the pressures you are sure to face. Knowing and acknowledging their presence should be of help in combatting them. Every day is a victory and every victory makes the struggle a little easier. The days become months and months become years and soon alcohol is a distant memory.

The new behaviors that were so strange and uncomfortable at first will become the normal way of life, and you will wonder how it could ever have been otherwise. Do you recall how you felt when your first love affair terminated? You were devastated and thought you would never recover, yet you did, and now perhaps have difficulty even remembering his or her name. The same will happen with your romance with alcohol. It, too, shall pass and become only a distant memory.

The human psyche is a complex thing, often so fragile in its reaction to slights, to loss of love or respect, so vulnerable to feelings of unworthiness and guilt, so weak in its acceptance of the inevitability of failure and doom. Yet a single flash of insight and determination may substitute for all that a strength and commitment of unbelievable proportions. The potential is there, waiting to be actuated, in most all people.

We all have different capacities for change, different learning abilities, different motivations, different drives, differ-ent data stored in our brains, but we share certain common needs. It is hoped that this book will help the person using alcohol to gain some insight into his potential for meeting these basic needs by more responsible behaviors and the strength and determination to pursue that potential.

It may come as a surprise to some to learn that indeed they have within themselves the power and ability to make changes in their behaviors that they had in the past believed to be beyond their control. In today's social environment we often seem to be immersed in a sea of victimhood. Most everyone seems to be a victim of something or other: racial or ethnic prejudice, poverty, physical disability, childhood sexual abuse, satanic ritual abuse, sexual harassment. One of the favorites is to blame parents for having abused or neglected one during childhood, a defense being successfully pleaded in a number of sordid criminal cases. Yet others who are severely physically or mentally handicapped, or have been horribly abused or neglected chose to take control of their lives and become worthwhile citizens, holding responsible positions, raising well adjusted families and living exemplary lives.

Morgan, one of my acquaintenances when I was in high school had a condition whereby any slight bump resulted in broken bones. He was usually confined to a wheelchair but learned to walk short distances using leg braces. He attended college although the braces wore bloody holes in his legs as he traveled from class to class. Eventually his knee joints solidified in a sitting position so that he was unable to straighten them. When I last saw him he was totally unable to move without assistance, had to be put to bed at night and dressed and placed in his chair in his home office each morning, had to brace his head with one hand while he answered the telephone with the other. But Morgan had earned his living as an accountant, had never asked for or received public assitance of any kind and, most important, didn't consider himself to be particularly handicapped. He was born with a severe physical problem through no fault of his but never considered himself a victim. He always spoke of the many wonderful things that had happened to him during his lifetime.

Most of us are more fortunate than Morgan, yet sometimes we squander our good health and good minds on substances that are disabling. We do so knowingly, often irresponsibly, sometimes merely seeking a thrill or new experience, frequently out of boredom or frustration. But it is nearly always done intentionally, and it is unrealistic to blame any one else. With equal determination you can reverse the process and discontinue the irresponsible behavior. But you must take the initiative. No one else can do it for you. And you are never too old or too young to take control.

If you are not yet ready to make this change, put this book aside in a convenient place, look at it once in a while, but keep it handy. Sooner or later you may experience a life crisis or reach a firm decision that you no longer will allow alcohol or other drugs to control your life and you then may commit yourself to taking control. This book is a self-help manual and designed to help you find the way.

NOTES

1. Saunders, Bill, Treatment Does Not Work: Some Criteria of Failure. In Heather, Nick et. al., *The Misuse of Alcohol: Crucial Issues in Dependence Treatment & Prevention.* (New York: New York University Press, 1985).

2. Riley, Diane M. et. al., Behavioral Treatment of Alcohol Problems: A Review and a Comparison of Behavioral and Nonbehavioral Studies. In Cox, W. Miles, ed., *Treatment and Prevention of Alcohol Problems: A Resource Manual.* (Orlando: Academic Press, Inc., 1987).

3. Ibid.

4. *Webster's Third New International Dictionary*, Gove, Philip Babcock, Ph.D., ed. (Springfield, Mass.: G. & C. Mirriam Co., 1976).

5. *Manual on Alcoholism,* American Medical Association, 1968, p 5.

6. *Webster's Third New International Dictionary.*

7. Clinebell, H. J., Jr. *Understanding and Counseling the Alcoholic.* (Nashville: Abingdon Press, 1968).

8. Jellinek, E. M., *The Disease Concept of Alcoholism.* (New Haven: Hillhouse Press, 1960).

9. Keller, M. and McCormick, M., *A Dictionary of Words About Alcohol.* (New Brunswick, N. J.: Rutgers Center of Alcohol Studies, 1968).

10. Robinson, David, *Talking Out of Alcoholism: The Self-Help Process of Alcoholics Anonymous.* (Baltimore, Md.: University Park Press, 1979).

11. Kissin, Benjamin, Medical Management of the Alcoholic Patient. In Kissin, Benjamin and Bagleiter, Henri, *The Biology of Alcoholism.* (New York: Plenum Press, 1977), Vol. 5, p 82.

12. Jellinek, E. M., Phases in the Drinking History of Alcoholics. *Quarterly Journal of Studies on Alcohol*, 1946, 71- 88.

13. Zimberg, Sheldon; Wallace, John; and Blume, Sheila B., *Practical Approaches to Alcoholism Psychotherapy.* (New York and London: Plenum Press, 1978).

14. Wilson, G. Terence, Alcoholism and Aversion Therapy: Issues, Ethics and Evidence. In Marlatt, G. Alan and Nathan, Peter E., eds., *Behavioral Approaches to Alcoholism.* (New Brunswick, N. J.:

Publications Division, Rutgers Center of Alcohol Studies, 1978).

15. Ibid.

16. Ibid.

17. Popular name for *Alcoholics Anonymous*, Third Edition, Alcoholics Anonymous World Service, Inc., 1939 (1976 Ed.)

18. Shore, Richard S. and Luce, John M., *To Your Health, the Pleasures, Problems, and Politics of Alcohol*. (N. Y.: Seabury Press, 1976), p 146 et seq.

19. Milt, Harry, *Alcoholism, Its Causes and Cure: A New Handbook*. (New York: Charles Scribner's Sons, 1976).

20. Kurtz, Ernest, *Not God: A History of Alcoholics Anony ous*. (Center City, Mn.: Hazelden Educational Service, 1979).

21. Ibid.

22. *Alcoholics Anonymous*, pp 58-60.

23. Ibid., p 60.

24. Ibid., pp 44-57.

25. Shore and Luce, *To your Health*.

26. *Alcoholics Anonymous*, p 564.

27. Kurtz, *Not God*, p 175 et seq. Kurtz describes evangelicalism, as the **announcement** of salvation as a gift from God, Pietist as the religious intuition struck first by man's **need** for salvation - by the goodness and power of the Divine.

28. Kurtz, *Not God*.

29. Leach, Barry, Does Alcoholics Anonymous Really Work? In Bourne, Peter G. and Fox, Ruth, *Alcoholism, Progress in Research and Treatment*. (N. Y. and London: Academic Press, 1973).

30. Blum, Eva Marie and Blum, Richard H., *Alcoholism, Modern Psychological Approaches to Treatment*. (San Francisco: Jossey-Bass, Inc., 1967). Also See McCrady, Barbara H. and Irvine, Sadi, Self-Help Groups. In Hester, Reid K. and Miller, William R., *Handbook of Alcoholism Treatment Approaches: Effective Alternatives*. (N. Y.: Pergamon Press, 1989), p 153-169.

31. Glasser, William, M. D., *Reality Therapy: A New Approach to Psychiatry*. (New York: Harper and Row, 1965).

32. Ibid., p 51-2 (Paraphrased for brevity).

33. Ibid., p 54 (Paraphrased for brevity).

34. Glasser, William., M. D., *Control Theory: A New Explanation of How We Control Our Lives* (New York: Harper and Row, 1984).

35. Sobell, Mark B. and Linda C., *Problem Drinkers: Guided Self-Change Treatment (N.Y & London: Guilford Press, 1993).*

36.   Ludwig, Arnold M., M. D., *Understanding the Alcoholic's Mind: The Nature of Craving and How to Control it.* (N.Y. and Oxford: Oxford University Press, 1988). p 16, 17.

GLOSSARY

AA: Alcoholics Anonymous, a self help agency for treatment of alcoholism.

Abstinence: Total self denial of alcohol in any form.

Al-Anon: Support group for spouses or significant others of alcoholics.

Alcoholics Anonymous: A self-help agency for the treatment of alcoholism.

Ambivalence: Uncertainty as to which attitude, approach or treatment to follow.

Anonymous: Having or giving no name.

BAC: Blood alcohol concentration.

Barbiturates: Acid or salt used as a sedative or hypnotic.

Basic needs: According to Glasser, the need to love and be loved and to feel we are worthwhile to ourselves and others.

Behavior therapy: Group of treatment techniques based on stimulus-response psychology.

Big Book: Popular name for the book, Alcoholics Anonymous.

Blacking out: Lack of awareness while seemingly conscious, after overindulgence in alcohol.

Blood alcohol concentration: Percentage of alcohol to total blood volume within the body.

Bottomed out: Point at which alcoholic acknowledges powerlessness over alcohol.

Caffeine: Stimulant and diuretic occurring in coffee, tea and kola nuts.

Chugging: Drinking of a container of alcohol without pause.

Cirrhosis: Chronic progressive disease of the liver, often resulting from alcohol abuse.

Cocaine: An alkaloid obtained from coca leaves, having first a stimulating, then a narcotic effect.

Conditioned response: Theory that one may be conditioned to respond predictably to a given stimulus.

Control theory: Glasser's theory on how living organisms control what happens to them.

Controlled drinking: Technique of learning to control alcohol consumption by monitoring.

Crack: Variety of cocaine.

Depressing: Glasserian concept that rather than getting depressed we choose to depress.

Disease concept: That alcoholism is a disease rather than a symptom of emotional maladjustment.

Drink Watchers: Self help organization devoted to controlled drinking.

Drunkalogues: Personal stories related by attendees at AA meetings.

Enabling: Actions of alcoholic's significant others that enable him to continue to abuse alcohol.

Enzymes: Living cells that act as catalysts in chemical reactions.

Euphoric: With feeling of well-being or elation.

Fermentation: Chemical change converting starches and sugars to alcohol.

Glasser, William, M.D.: Noted psychiatrist and author of Reality Therapy and other books.

Hallucinations: Perception of objects that are not really there.

Hangover: Disagreeable aftereffects of overindulgence in alcohol.

Heroin: A highly addictive narcotic made from morphine.

Higher Power: In AA circles, "God, as we understand him".

Intervention: Technique intended to interrupt alcoholic's drinking cycle.

Life crisis: Occurrence of uncommon significance, frequently resulting in dramatic life changes.

LSD: Lysergic acid diethylamide, compound that causes psychotic symptoms similar to schizophrenia.

Mandate: Order, usually judicial.

Marijuana: Dried leaves and flowering tops of hemp plant, smoked for intoxicating effect.

Metabolism: Process by which a substance is assimilated by the body.

Methamphetamine: Stimulant of central nervous system, often used in treatment of obesity.

Milieu: Setting or environment.

Modality: Method.

Monitoring: Keeping accurate record of alcohol consumption.

Multiple addiction: Addiction to more than one mind altering drug at the same time.

Near beer: A beverage that tastes like beer but contains only one half of 1% alcohol.

Negative reinforcement: Encouragement of desirable behavior by punishment or threat thereof.

Nicotine: Poisonous volatile alkaloid occurring in tobacco.

One day at a time: AA concept that one must commit to sobriety only for today.

Open meetings: AA meetings that may be attended by anyone, alcoholic or not.

Personal world: The world as each person perceives it.

Positive reinforcement: Encouragement of desirable conduct by granting of rewards.

Progression concept: That problem drinking inevitably leads to alcoholism.

Real world: The world as it really exists.

Reality Therapy: William Glasser's new approach to psychotherapy.

Relapse: Return to drinking after a period of sobriety.

Significant Other: Person of great importance in your life.

Slip: Relapse. Return to drinking after a period of sobriety.

Spontaneous remission: Recovery without apparent cause.

Stupor: Absence of spontaneous movement - impaired consciousness.

Twelve steps: The twelve guiding steps of AA.

Twelve traditions: How AA feels it can best stay whole and survive.

Valium: Common muscle relaxant and tranquilizer.

Working the program: Following the twelve steps and observing the twelve traditions of AA.

Index

122